Shattering
THE
GLASS SLIPPER

Destroying Fairy-Tale Thinking
Before It Destroys You

Charles W. Marshall

 Prominent
Publishing

Shattering the Glass Slipper
Copyright © 2002 by Charles W. Marshall

ISBN 0-9748084-5-8

Contact:
M Power Resources, LLC
www.MPowerResources.com
info@MPowerResources.com

Edited by Laura A. Marshall
Cover design by Tommy Wood, Stimulus, Inc.
Printed in the United States of America

*To the Cinderellas of this world who
await the arrival of the magic.*

Table of Contents

ACKNOWLEDGEMENTS

In my life I have been the recipient of much unwarranted favor at the hands of people who chose to give of themselves for my betterment. It was through these people that I first learned to develop and implement the Seven Powers.

I would like to extend my sincere, heartfelt appreciation to the following people:

My junior high school band instructor, Thad Mullins, believed in me and encouraged me to pursue my passion for music, when few others saw anything in me that would inspire confidence. I've spoken publicly countless times about the impact Mr. Mullins made in my life by exercising the Power of Belief, but I only recently remembered that he possessed a severe speech disability. How insignificant that now seems in comparison to the impact he made in my life.

H. Aaron Meyers of the Tom James Company was one of my first (and best) sales managers who took a huge leap of faith in hiring me for a sales position early in my career. Aaron tirelessly invested in my career, mind, and soul without ever seeing a personal or business return in his investment. He amazed me with his proficiency in exercising the Power of

Vision and, in my mind, represents the Power of Character as few others do. In short, he is one of the finest men I've ever had the pleasure of knowing.

Pastor Jack Wolfe is a friend, board member, advisor, and mentor. He embodies so many of the Seven Powers, it is difficult to select any one or two that he best represents. He has consistently employed the Power of Belief like very few others have. He has exemplified the Power of Failure, harnessing it and using its momentum to propel him toward his next objective. He also represents to me the embodiment of the Power of Character. This world is a better place for having him in it. On that great day when he meets our Master face to face, he will surely be one to whom it is said, "Well done, thou good and faithful servant."

Fred and Gwen Marshall, my father and mother, who have now passed from this life to the next, were the first to instill in me a belief that I could achieve my dreams. They were the first to counsel me to action, rather than complacency. They were the first to insist that I use and develop my Power of Mind. Although they certainly were not perfect, I believe I understand them much better now that I walk the same path as they did as parent and provider.

My bride, Laura Marshall, is my friend and companion on this often merry and sometimes perilous adventure of life. This book would not have been possible without her generously contributing her time, advice, expertise, and encouragement. She is my constant in an inconsistent and turbulent world. Her steadfast love, abundant wisdom, and endless effort have helped me navigate through victory and heartbreak alike. Laura, once again, thanks for saying "yes."

My daughter, Faith, arrived in February 2002 and, in one moment, forever changed my priorities and passions. Thank you, little one, for making me a daddy.

Many newspapers and publications have been so kind as to carry *M-Powered Living*, my motivational column. I thank you all for helping me to encourage individuals to achieve their potential.

Throughout the years, a great many companies and organizations have graciously permitted me to speak to their groups. I count it an honor whenever I am allowed to share the principles that I believe in so deeply.

And finally, it would be absurd, when embarking upon any creative effort, not to express gratitude to the God of all creation, in whose image we are made and from whom all creation emanates. The true adventure in life is the continual discovery of him and his love for mankind.

INTRODUCTION

Once upon a time there lived a person who sat reading this book (perhaps the very one that holds it now). Until this time, his life had been filled with mediocrity, along with a measure of failure. In all probability, his mind had been infected with a virus.

Just as your body can have a virus, so can your thinking. Not a biological virus, nor a chemical imbalance, both which affect the brain itself, but a psychological virus that infects your rationale and reason. Similar to a computer that becomes infected with a virus and is rendered inoperable and useless, so a mind can also have its proper functions hampered or damaged by the virus of faulty thinking.

Like all viruses, this one possesses an aggressive nature and a strong proclivity to flourish and spread. It viciously attacks its host, never resting until it has done its work. It infects our government, hinders our economy, cripples our education system, and incapacitates our businesses. It has infected countless individuals and relationships, all the while going undetected and unheeded.

Millions of people suffer from this malady and never even know it. The fact that this virus is so prevalent has rendered it almost undetectable. People are unable to see the woods for the trees. Because it is everywhere, it is considered normal to have this faulty rationale, and anyone who thinks otherwise is often misunderstood and scorned.

This virus is called fairy-tale thinking. Its symptoms are fantasizing, irrational expectations, inactivity, and misplaced effort. It always results in frustration, confusion, anger, hopelessness, and ultimately, a wasted life.

Fairy-tale thinking is the philosophical belief that someday, without our doing anything, something wonderful is going to happen that will allow us to live happily ever after. This idea is first implanted into our minds in our youth from numerous fairy tales such as *Cinderella, Sleeping Beauty, Little Red Riding Hood, Goldilocks and the Three Bears*, and many more.

The basic premise of most fairy tales is that the protagonist (usually female) falls into in an unhappy or dangerous situation only to be rescued by an outside agency such as a handsome prince, white knight, or even just dumb luck.

This philosophy is perpetuated into our adulthood by countless movies, television shows, books, and magazines. We hunger for these stories because they offer hope of a better day and a brighter tomorrow. It is easier to bear today's burden if we believe tomorrow is going to be better.

So what is wrong with hope? Are all fairy tales bad?

Fairy tales are certainly not evil, but they do espouse an unhealthy philosophy and offer false hope which will destroy your relationships, ruin your health, and decimate your finances.

People infected with the fairy-tale virus believe that some-day someone is going to touch them with a magic wand, changing their life forever because they deserve it. They believe deep within their hearts that some indefinable some-thing will deliver them from their misery and elevate them to success in business, love, or health because they have been good. They think if they just keep sweeping up the cinders and submissively tending house (business, job, relationship, etc.), that heaven will smile on them and their servitude will be rewarded.

And so they wait. And then they wait some more.

Fairy-tale thinking is often misdiagnosed as laziness or apathy because it results in reduced effort. Employees with this mindset don't take ownership of their jobs, doing just enough to get by. They have no emotional investment because within their thinking lies the belief that one day their ship will come in. Until then, they tread water. Why swim for shore if a boat is on the way?

People with fairy-tale thinking always have trouble with romantic relationships. They either spend their lives forever searching for the perfect Prince (or Princess) Charming, or they marry someone they believe is Prince or Princess Charming, only to be disappointed later. People who base their relationships on fairy-tale thinking are always disap-pointed because they believe that a perfect person exists whose purpose is to rescue them and make them happy.

Business leaders with fairy-tale thinking focus their company's efforts on the big deal, rather than on developing growth strategies or building their organizational leadership. Their judgment is usually impaired and their efforts misplaced.

They either spend too much, investing in do-or-die, all-or-nothing endeavors, or they fail to risk any capital at all, thinking that something good is bound to happen soon if they just keep "being good."

Unfortunately, people infected with fairy-tale thinking are rarely ever cured because the virus usually remains undetected. Until the very end, the victims often still think that unnamed "something" will come along. Or, recognizing that their philosophy didn't yield the expected payoff, they blame bad luck, still recalling the times when they almost got that big break.

How about you? Have you been waiting all your life for something wonderful to happen? Have you dreamed of one day striking it rich or finding that perfect someone? Have you been treading water instead of swimming for shore?

Perhaps a better question might be, what would it take for you to exchange your fairy-tale thinking for another philosophy?

Are you waiting for a sign? If it is a sign you desire, then accept this book as that sign. Accept that somehow, you were meant to read this book and it was meant to be the impetus you need to make a new beginning. Accept that the omen you have awaited all your life has finally arrived in the form of a book. Let it be your starting point for now. Let that be your incentive to go on reading until you can find better reasons to support entertaining a different philosophy other than the one you have held for so long.

It won't be easy. No virus abandons its host without a battle. The good news is that fairy-tale thinking is easy to identify (once you know what to look for) and can be successfully treated.

The first step toward recovery is for the victim to realize that real life is not a fairy tale. The world just does not work that way. Real life isn't the achievement of one big objective and then retiring to live "happily ever after." Fairy-tale thinkers will always resist this truth because they think of success as a destination.

"I'd be happy if I were married."

"I wish I would win the lottery!"

"If I had a million (billion, hundred-thousand) dollars, then I'd be successful."

"I wish I were a movie star."

"I'd be happy if I had a different job."

Fairy-tale thinkers often build their definition of success on such vague concepts as happiness or wealth. Such intangible terms have relative meanings and are thus elusive and unattainable. When your life's goal is to be happy or rich, you will always feel defeated and frustrated because you are aiming for a shifting mirage that changes based on perspective, mood, and socioeconomic status.

The real-world truth is that success is not a dollar amount nor a relationship. Success is not the attainment of a thing or an enviable position. Nor is it recognition or a life of ease.

Think of success, rather, in terms of becoming. Think of it as the completion of each leg of a never-ending journey.

This is not to say that success is synonymous with the journey itself. Everyone is journeying through life, but everyone is certainly not successful. There is nothing commendable about simply journeying through life. One can stand perfectly still on the conveyor belt of life and still travel from one end to the other with no effort or success whatsoever.

No, only he is successful who makes marked, specific progress toward the achievement of growth, strength, and stability in the areas of finance, emotion, spirit, body, and mind. There is no one destination called success. There is no one point of arrival, but many steps that lead to more growth, challenge, and victory.

If one were to draw a line on a chart representing the journey of any successful person, it would never be a straight line rising from poverty to wealth, from loneliness to relationship, from obscurity to fame. It would always be a series of victories followed by successive failures, resembling more a stairway than a straight incline.

Once again, there is no unalterable state of happiness and wealth where you may arrive and expect to dwell for the rest of your life. Therefore, when you find yourself in a position of poverty or dissatisfaction, do not automatically classify yourself as a failure. It might very well be that you are in one of the many necessary stages of growth on the way to your next victory.

Only he is a failure who has surrendered to an existence of mediocrity and subservience. Do not think of success as the realization of a level of material or emotional gain, but as progress. Stop thinking in terms of success versus failure, but rather as progress versus stagnation. Are you moving (in the right direction) or are you stagnate? Are you taking steps, however small, or have you given up?

In just such a small act as reading this book, you are demonstrating that you have both the ability and the initiative to drive fairy-tale thinking, along with all of its symptoms, from your life.

But just a word or two of warning: This book is not magical and will not give you success.

To achieve success, one must change the way one thinks, and that is only accomplished after reading many books and implementing the ideas found therein.

This book, rather, is the beginning of your success as you divest yourself of the Three Deceptions, employ the Seven Powers, and guard against the Five Deadly Enemies. When you commit to the pursuit of personal growth, success cannot be far behind.

Nor is this a how-to book. It will not offer you "the secret formula for success in relationships" or "the four easy steps to prosperity." It will not tell you what one thing you should do for instantaneous wealth. It will not tell you what stock to invest in or what type of business to begin.

If you are waiting for someone to tell you what to do, you are not accessing the tremendous resources that lie within you. You are waiting for your fairy godmother. Looking for someone to give you all the answers is just another way of saying you are waiting for someone to touch you with a magic wand.

You must learn not to look to anyone for your success. Instead, you must examine your thinking, scouring your habits and inclinations for any symptoms of the fairy-tale virus. As you read this book, any traces of fairy-tale thinking in your life will become increasingly obvious. By the end of the book, not only should you be able to properly diagnose any diseased thinking you have, but you will be aware of the immense power you have to conquer this illness.

What this book offers is a diagnosis, treatment plan, and inoculation against any further attacks of the fairy-tale virus.

But the treatment itself will be up to you. Don't turn back. Do not heed the call of complacency. Success calls your name and beckons you forward. You have been awaiting this moment your entire life.

This is your beginning. This is your sign.

PART I

Cinderella Retold

1

CINDERELLA RETOLD

Once upon a time, in a land far away and long forgotten, there lived a maiden with her wicked stepmother and two wicked stepsisters. The maiden distinguished herself neither in beauty, intelligence, nor talent, but nonetheless was virtuous and good; more so in that she was cruelly treated by her wicked stepmother and stepsisters.

Daily they would hurl insults at the poor girl and missed no opportunity of humiliating her. What little food they gave her she was made to eat apart from the family, being deemed unworthy to sit with them. She was forced to wear clothes that were little more than rags. In the winter, she was given no coat and would shiver violently as she walked through the marketplace, warmed only by the shame she felt in her poverty.

Her stepmother, being of a base and corrupt nature, was exceedingly harsh and delighted in forcing the girl to undertake countless tasks of the most menial sort. One of the worst was her daily chore of scrubbing the fireplace, in which she became, in the course of the task, covered from head to toe with soot and cinders. It was thus that they began to call her Cinderella.

All the while Cinderella bravely endured the hardship, thinking that one day her life would change—that one day something magical would happen to rescue her from this dismal existence. She longed for a different life, one of respect and fulfillment; to wear nice clothes, to eat good food, to not be ashamed to be seen in public. She also longed for love. She dreamed of one day finding Mr. Right, a Prince Charming who, perhaps, might one day recognize her worth and rescue her from all the unpleasantness in her life.

But Cinderella was not without hope. For, just before her real mother died, she told Cinderella that if she were only good, she would one day be rewarded. And so it was that day after day Cinderella courageously suffered in silence while continuing to harbor a vague hope that one day, maybe one day soon, her ship would come in.

Then one day an envelope with gold lettering arrived at the cottage. Cinderella's stepmother and stepsisters squealed with delight as they tore open the envelope which contained an invitation to the royal ball to be held at the palace in honor of the prince. The prince had recently come of age and it was rumored that he would soon take a bride. Perhaps, thought the stepmother, that bride might be one of her very own daughters, and she envisioned herself living in opulence and grandeur at the royal palace.

Immediately the house began to bustle with excitement as the preparations were made for the ball. Cinderella spent many hours sewing the dresses of her stepsisters and then sewing them again after her stepsisters tore them to pieces, finding the most minuscule fault with them.

Cinderella had asked if she might also attend the royal ball but was roundly and flatly refused. How could she, they asked—a mere servant-girl with no means, no dress, and no conveyance—attend a ball? No, no, they laughed. Her time would be far better spent helping her stepsisters instead.

But deep in her heart Cinderella still hoped. Maybe something magical would happen. Maybe somehow, some way, something would happen so that all her dreams would come true. Perhaps she would go to the ball. Perhaps the prince would fall in love with her. Perhaps he would insist on marrying her and punish all those who had been so cruel to her.

Finally the night of the ball arrived. After seeing her step-mother and stepsisters get into the carriage and leave for the ball, Cinderella went up to her attic bedroom and cried. She wondered why good things never seemed to happen to her. Why was it always the other people, even the wicked people, that got all the luck?

But still she had hope. She felt deeply in her heart that if she were good enough and suffered bravely, she would one day be rewarded. Perhaps, she thought, she had not suffered enough. Maybe to truly deserve the good things in life she must suffer more. But no, her stepfamily had suffered very little, yet they had so much.

And so she waited. The evening is young, she reasoned. Anything might still happen. There might still be time to attend the ball at the royal palace, she thought. And so she waited some more. She lay on her bed and dreamed of the wonderful night she might have at the prince's ball. She envisioned herself in a beautiful gown and sparkling jewels.

She awoke in the dark to the sound of the front door closing and the loud laughter of her stepfamily. Why had they come back so early? Did they forget something? But no. The candle had burned completely out and the moon had risen high in the sky. Was it possible? Had she fallen asleep and missed the ball?

That was exactly what had happened! She sat in stunned silence as she heard her stepfamily recount their favorite parts of the evening. Both girls had actually danced with the prince and had received an invitation to return to the castle!

The next day, everything was much the same for Cinderella. She did the same chores, wore the same clothes, and ate the same sort of food. She endured the same insults from her stepmother and stepsisters as before, yet now it was even more bitter because of the knowledge that they had attended the ball and lived the dream—yes, her dream.

For the first time in her life, she began to realize that it was possible, even probable, that she would live in the manner in which she now suffered for the rest of her life.

This thought depressed her greatly. Still, at times she was able to retreat into the blissful world of fantasy in which she and her prince would someday meet and fall madly in love. But now this fantasy seemed thinner and less real than it had before. Now she would shake herself out of her daydreams and disgustedly chide herself for her foolish notions.

Now that she had experienced such a bitter disappointment, suffering bravely no longer seemed attractive and reasonable, since it no longer promised an eventual reward. To the burden of her labor was added the burden of drudgery so that all her days were filled with misery. Why hadn't the magic come? Why hadn't she been the one? Didn't she deserve it? Didn't heaven care? Was her life just a meaningless exercise in futility?

One day as she shuffled through the marketplace with her head cast down and shoulders drooping, she caught the eye of a wealthy old merchant. The merchant was dressed in fine clothing, rode in an ornate carriage, and was just returning from the palace, having concluded some very important and profitable trade negotiations.

As he looked out of his carriage, he saw Cinderella and the kindness of his heart bade him order the carriage to stop. He had his servant summon Cinderella to his carriage and she was invited to sit inside.

There, the merchant offered her food and drink such as she could not remember tasting. After she was refreshed, he asked her why a young girl such as herself was so downcast.

At this expression of concern, Cinderella burst into tears, for it had been a very long time since anyone had pitied her and shown her such compassion. At first haltingly, and then in a flood, she poured out her whole tale, omitting no detail, however small.

The old merchant sat listening intently, nodded his head, and every now and then asked a clarifying question. When she finished, Cinderella felt embarrassed at her show of emotion and made to get out of the carriage, but the old merchant begged her to stay and asked leave to relate a bit of his own tale.

He told her he too had once been a slave, and that he also longed for a magical deliverance from his situation, but nothing ever happened. He related how he fell further and further into despondency and began playing games of chance, losing what little money he then possessed. He began to partake of drink so as to forget his misery by drunkenness. But all of this only made his life more miserable.

Then one day, he happened to meet a wealthy man much in the same way he had met Cinderella.

"Did the rich man give you riches, jewels, and fine clothing?" blurted Cinderella before she had a chance to think.

"No," said the old merchant. "He gave me something far more valuable—something I am going to give to you now."

Saying this, the old man reached into his bag. Cinderella leaned forward, her hands clasped and her eyes shining, as she eagerly awaited the magnificent treasure the wealthy merchant was to give her. The smile quickly faded from her face, though, when she saw what it was.

From the bag he had taken an old, thoroughly worn, small brown book. As he looked at it, a faint smile danced upon his lips and he seemed lost in thought as he gently caressed the cover.

"It's, um, a book?" asked Cinderella.

"No, no, no!" said the wealthy merchant. "It's not a book. It's THE *Book of Success*."

Cinderella took the book from the old man and sat in stunned silence. Was the old man making sport of her? Was this an elaborate practical joke? If so, the old man didn't seem to know it. He sat there, beaming, as though he had just presented her with his most valuable possession, for indeed it was.

Perhaps the old man has lost his mind, thought Cinderella. She touched his hand, mumbled a few words of gratitude, and once again started to leave the carriage.

"You mustn't leave just yet," said the old man, motioning her to sit again. "I haven't finished telling you my story.

"After I received the book," he began again, as Cinderella regained her seat, "I did not read it for a long while. One day, not having anything better to do, I picked it up and began reading. I was skeptical at first, but then, perhaps out of desperation or perhaps from boredom—I do not know which—I began to practice the principles of this book and apply them to my life.

"It would be a long and weary tale indeed for a young woman such as yourself to endure if I were to relate my entire journey, but suffice to say, that after much hardship and many years of toil, I not only gained my independence, but have become very wealthy.

"Not all who have read this book have succeeded as I have, nor will all who read it in the future. But I can say that those who read this book and are careful to apply its principles will assuredly improve their situation and find the road to success."

After once again thanking the wealthy old merchant, Cinderella left the carriage and walked home. She read the book late into the evening and then reread it the following day. The book was not a magical book, but it seemed as though it were written directly to her. Not just *for* her but *to* Cinderella herself. As she read the book, at times she was angered, as it conflicted with the principles upon which she had hitherto built her life. Other times she was astounded at the simplicity of the concepts. She wept as she read about the Three Deceptions. She felt encouraged and emboldened as she read about the Seven Powers, and she grew stern and resolved when she read of the Five Deadly Enemies.

At this point, Cinderella began the battle for her life. She had already come to the realization that without change she was doomed to be a prisoner forever, so she was ready to begin.

Soon, as she began to practice the principles of the book, her stepmother and stepsisters began to notice a difference in Cinderella. She seemed more self-assured. She had more direction. She had always worked hard, but now her work was focused.

With the meager savings she had, she began to trade in the market and soon had a small business. This, of course, angered her stepfamily greatly, and she was thrown out of their house. This bothered Cinderella little as she had planned to move soon anyway. She rented a small room with her earnings and continued to study and apply the principles of the *Book of Success*.

After some time had passed, she opened a store of her own, and then another. In the meantime, she met a like-minded, capable young man, married, and had children. Eventually, she sold her businesses at a profit, started another business, and then another.

After many years had passed, Cinderella had lived to be a very old woman and had achieved all that she had desired. As she rode through the village one day, remembering all she had experienced, a profound gratitude welled within her heart for the small, worn book the old man had given her years before.

She now held the book in her withered, old hands, thinking of how the old merchant had treasured the book and how she had come to value it herself. It was at that moment that she looked out of her carriage and saw a young man dressed in rags with a sad and weary expression on his face. He carried only a small burden over his shoulder, but seemed as though he also carried the weight of disappointment and hardship.

Cinderella ordered her driver to pull to the curb and smiled as she had the young man summoned to the carriage.

PART II

The Book of Success

THE THREE DECEPTIONS

Y ou have been deceived. For a while this deception may have been acceptable, or even enjoyable, but if you are now reading this book, perhaps you have come to the realization that things are not always as they seem. Sometimes what appears to be good in your life is really killing you. If you are to break the pattern, it is time you were honest with yourself and confronted reality.

Reality is what the world really is. Fantasy is what you would like the world to be. In order to obtain success, you must accept what your world is and work toward what you would like it to be. It's that simple.

Unfortunately, many people choose to live in a fantasy world of dreams and illusion. Subconsciously, they would prefer to live in a fairy-tale world and are frustrated when life doesn't behave in accordance with these preconceptions. These people do not want to hear the truth. They would cover their ears and insist upon continuing in ignorance. They are victims of the virus of fairy-tale thinking. It is said that ignorance is bliss, but ignorance of the truth often means a lifetime of hardship and heartbreak.

Not everyone is ready, or desires, to face reality. They believe it is easier to sleep in ignorance than to wake to knowledge. Knowledge demands action. Therefore, many people choose to live in deception and may never wake to realize the richness of the life they have unwittingly lost.

There are three basic deceptions which cause people to fail. To reveal these deceptions is to unmask an enemy—an enemy which seeks your very life—an enemy that would have you waste your entire life waiting in frustration, disappointment, and despair.

The main danger of the Three Deceptions is that if you are either consciously or subconsciously depending on them, then you are not going to be actively developing and strengthening the Seven Powers in your life. The Seven Powers represent a limitless reservoir of strength from which you can draw so that you can tackle any problem. Believing in the Three Deceptions will only weaken you as you let your Seven Powers atrophy.

As you read the Three Deceptions, search out the fairy-tale virus in your life. Seek it wherever it may lie. Does it hide in your romantic life? Does it lie in your finances? Maybe it disguises itself buried in your religious beliefs or lack thereof. Only you can uncover its hiding places. Only you can root it out and expel it from your life.

2

THE DECEPTION OF MAGIC

$\mathfrak{R}$ ead these words carefully: There is no magic. There is no magic wand. There is no fairy godmother.

This is not to say that there is no unseen or supernatural world, but that there is no mystical force in the universe whose sole purpose is to make you successful in any given area of your life.

How many people now live with the vague, yet very real, hope buried somewhere deep within them that one day their ship is going to come in? How many young people dream of fortune and fame in theater, music, and sports? How many people are hoping to find the perfect mate? How many adults dream of wealth and prestige if only they could win a lottery, get that big promotion, or receive an inheritance?

Such people laugh and tell themselves that they aren't really serious about such notions, that such ideas are merely fancies of theirs. But their actions betray them when they behave as though it will only be a matter of time before *it* happens. The salesman who barely works but hopes for that one big deal; the young man working countless dead-end jobs; the old woman spending her income in various forms of gambling; the middle-aged man living all by himself, never daring romance—all waiting for and dreaming of a glory they will never see.

There are those who are now reading these words, who are crying, "How do you know my dreams will never come true? Who says they won't?"

There is nothing special, unique, or magical about dreams. If everyone who had dreams were to realize them, then everyone in the world would be rich, happy, and healthy, but not everyone is. All have dreams, but not all are successful. Unless dreams are transformed into something else entirely, they will always remain just dreams. Unless one utilizes the Seven Powers, one's dreams will remain mere flights of fancy.

> *Unless dreams are transformed into something else entirely, they will always remain just dreams.*

Whenever you see a singer or an actor who has seemingly risen to stardom overnight, do not be deceived. There is no such thing as overnight success. When you see such a person, you are not looking at the result of a magical rise to success. You are looking at years of hard work, training, and sacrifice. Even when an individual does achieve wealth and recognition at a young age, it is not by chance. No, behind every star there is a wealth of other people working behind the scenes who have developed business and marketing systems designed to capitalize on that performer's talent and ability.

Invariably, there comes a day in the lives of most dreamers when they wake up and wonder why nothing ever happened to them. They were waiting for magic that never happened. They were waiting to be discovered. They were waiting for Mr. or Ms. Perfect. They were waiting for the big win or the one sale that would catapult them to riches and notoriety. But it never happened, and never will, unless hard changes are made.

Some of the spiritually-minded attempt to redeem these beliefs by claiming that God will one day bless them, without their having lifted a finger. When nothing happens, their disappointment is severe, usually resulting in acute disillusionment and a falling away from their faith. Ultimately, they blame God for their own failure. But you should know that heaven does indeed offer help to those willing to look in that direction, but only through the application of the Seven Powers.

Here on earth, the harsh, hard reality is that there is no magic. Get it into your mind. Never again allow yourself to believe that "it will all work out somehow," or that "it will all turn out all right." It won't. That's fairy-tale thinking, and it is a recipe for failure, disaster, and disappointment.

3

THE DECEPTION OF SOMEDAY

o you believe in "someday"? Are you thinking that someday you'll be rich, someday you'll save some money, someday you'll find the right person, someday you'll lose weight?

Those who believe in "someday" are fairy-tale thinkers
who believe that "someday" is when the magic finally arrives.
They wait for it like children waiting for Christmas morning.
They believe "someday" is a magical day, sometime in the
future, when happiness will finally be theirs and their dreams
will finally come true. They repeat their mantra of failure
over and over in the back of their minds, believing it with all
of their hearts.

> "Someday I'm going to really get serious about my
> career."
> "Someday I'm going to start eating right."
> "Someday I'm going to start my own business."
> "Someday the right one will come along."
> "Someday I'm going to quit this lousy job."
> "Someday I'm going to learn to play an instrument."

But little do they know that "someday" only comes as an
enemy, and never as a friend. Those who believe in the
magic of "someday" are always surprised that it doesn't

look anything like they thought it would. Suddenly they're much older and no farther down the road toward their dreams. They realize far too late that they spent their lives waiting for a "someday" that wasn't their friend, after all.

The danger of waiting for the happiness of "someday" is that it distracts you from seeking happiness in your present situation today. Too many people are willing to endure misery today, because they think "someday" will bring them fulfillment.

They stay in relationships with people who have no intention of marrying them. They stay at jobs with no possibility for advancement. They live in areas they really don't like. All because they're waiting for the magic to arrive "someday."

> *The danger of waiting for the happiness of "someday" is that it distracts you from seeking happiness in your present situation today.*

The truth is, that type of someday will never arrive.

Those who employ the Seven Powers never think "someday" will rescue them. They are constantly working to defeat "someday." They take time into consideration by realizing that the clock is running and that time waits for no one. We all get one life and this is it.

They also are aware that there is no "happily ever after." Real life always continues and the story never ends. There never is a place in any life where all struggle stops and happiness is a perpetual state. Sometimes there are seasons of respite from struggle, but those are usually all too brief, and shortly a new trial arises.

Those who believe in "someday" define success as some mystical point in time when all problems disappear and they finally have *enough*. They tell themselves that they don't want to be rich. Not really. They just want enough. But what they haven't learned is that "enough" is a relative term and is always changing. It never stays the same, so that what seems enough to you today, will not seem enough tomorrow. As your wealth increases, so do your financial responsibilities.

You might define success as living in that special neighborhood and believe you will finally have enough when you are there. But when you get there, your definition of enough will change again, because there is always a better neighborhood somewhere else. There is always someone else who has a better relationship, job, or lifestyle. "Enough" is an illusion.

Even so, there are those who would cling to a "someday" that will never arrive. They pathetically waste their enormous potential by remaining dormant, waiting for a mirage. They sincerely believe that "someday" will come and their lives will be changed. But it does not matter that they are sincere, because they are sincerely wrong. The strength of one's conviction does not turn a lie into the truth.

If you are to wield the Seven Powers, you must discard the deception of "someday." Throw away the notion that things will get better and "it will turn out all right" without your doing anything to change the situation or yourself. Shed the belief that good things will happen to you just because you waited for them.

"Someday" will only betray and disappoint you. Divorce yourself from your trust in it.

THE DECEPTION OF ENTITLEMENT

Perhaps the most dangerous of the Three Deceptions is the Deception of Entitlement, for it plays to the weakest aspect of our humanity—our love of ourselves.

Beneath all our insecurities and doubts, all of us believe that we are special, and the truth is, we are. Each of us is unique. Each of us is an irreplaceable individual with his own unique set of gifts and talents. But this wonderful sense of self-worth can become warped so that we believe that worth equals privilege. We can come to believe that somehow we have a right to have good things in our lives.

The person with entitlement thinking is often frustrated and angry. He has the sense that life has somehow cheated him. He thinks that success is his due because he has been "good" or is a "nice" person.

> "Why don't I have money (...a girlfriend ...a better
> job ...a nicer house)?"
> "When is it going to be my turn?"
> "Haven't I suffered long enough?"
> "Why does Jim get all the breaks? It's not fair!"
> "Why do all the good things happen to other people?"

The underlying foundation of an entitlement mindset is

fairy-tale thinking. A person with an entitlement mindset believes that only luck stands between him and success. Because of this, he is a slave to fear because it only makes sense that what can be given can also be taken away.

The same person that demands a yearly raise simply because he showed up at work and did only that which was required of him also lives in fear that he may be fired. He thinks his company exists to provide him with a job and that a paycheck is his right. He feels indignant and threatened if it is suggested that his company might no longer need his services.

People with an entitlement mindset feel that a serious, romantic relationship is a mystical, cosmic occurrence that happens to a select, happy few. They can't understand why they never have a date. It never occurs to them that to find a good mate, they must first be a good prospect themselves. They refuse to alter their appearance, habits, or personality because they say they want someone to love them as they are, never realizing or admitting that they are unwilling to accept someone else on the same terms. They feel that one day true love will come along because they are so special.

But the untold truth about entitlement thinking is that it weakens, not strengthens, your chances for success. It weakens them because, if you are waiting for your turn or for someone else to give you a break, you won't take the necessary steps that will lead you to success. You will be stuck in a repetitive pattern of dependence on a break that will never materialize.

The greatest hazard of entitlement thinking is that it robs you of ownership—not only the ownership of the spoils of success, but far more important, the ownership of achievement. It robs you of the power of knowing that you placed yourself in the position of success and therefore can do it again if need be. It robs you of the confidence needed to translate your present success into a greater success. It robs you of the resolve needed to take risks.

Entitlement is having something handed to you, either through luck or charity. When you achieve something yourself, by using your own creativity and effort, you know that no one else gave it to you and therefore your sense of self-worth increases.

> *The greatest hazard of entitlement thinking is that it robs you of ownership—not only the ownership of the spoils of success, but far more important, the ownership of achievement.*

Entitlement thinking weakens you and makes you its prisoner. Once you subjugate yourself to entitlement thinking, you become a prisoner of the fear of losing your meager benefits. You are a slave who is afraid to leave your cruel master because you fear not having the means to support yourself if you were free.

And that is the bargain you have made with yourself. You tell yourself you will wait for your break, for your share, for Lady Luck to smile upon you and give you your due. In return, you settle for the bondage that is a life of frustration, fear, and lack.

How do you escape the trap of entitlement thinking? By realizing and embracing one basic truth: No one owes you anything. If you are a grown adult, no one is responsible for taking care of you. Do you hear the voices in your mind rising to object? What if such and such is the case? But what about...? But in some cases...?

You must firmly walk away from all such thinking if you are to be free. Entitlement does not give up its slaves willingly. It will be a fight, and the prize is your life.

THE SEVEN POWERS

𝕯 o you hear that tiny voice? It's the one beneath all the other voices in your mind. Underneath the other voices that tell you that you will never become anything, that, for one reason or another, you are of little value. Underneath the doubt and fear. Underneath the skepticism and excuses.

Maybe you can't even hear that small voice anymore. Maybe you have long since forgotten it. Maybe that's why you wait for magic in your life. Maybe it's easier to believe in magic than to contemplate a lifetime full of need and unfulfilled desire.

But this voice is different. This voice tells you that you were meant for more. It says that you were not meant to live a life of deficiency, that you were meant to enjoy an abundance. It tells you that you are special and destined for great things.

Could it be? If this is so, then why haven't you experienced it? Are such things as wealth and love just meant for the select few? Has this universe laid out a complicated system where the chosen few receive blessing after blessing, and the rest suffer in deprivation?

Have you ever felt like one of the "have-nots"? Have you

been told you are not good-looking enough, smart enough, or young enough? Have you been told that you don't have the right clothes, live in the right house, or have the right qualifications? Maybe you didn't attend the right school. Maybe others don't think you're tall enough. Maybe they don't think your skin is the "right" color. Is your nose too big? Do you weigh too much? Are you too thin? Do you feel it's just too late for you to succeed?

Are there really some people who just have what it takes to be successful—that are gifted from birth and bound for success? There are indeed. As a matter of fact, you know such a person. This individual possesses everything needed to experience the fullness that this life has to offer. This person possesses special powers that offer the possibility of success, no matter what the circumstance. This person is you!

Are you able to believe that you now possess everything that you need to begin a life of triumph and accomplishment? Can you picture such a "you"?

At this point, people usually start to think one of two very different things. They either immediately slip into fairy-tale thinking, saying to themselves, "Yes, I believe what you are saying. I knew I was special. I knew that one day something wonderful would happen to me and am waiting for it now!"

Or they think, "I know better. Such things don't exist. This is just another form of positive thinking. I've tried that, and it doesn't work."

Both conclusions are as far away from the truth as can be.

As you read the following pages, try to keep your mind free of such prejudices and allow yourself to explore the possibility that you now possess undiscovered secret powers which, as you access and engage them, have the capability to revolutionize your life and bring you success.

The Seven Powers have no magic in them, and control over them does not come easily. Nor will any single one of the Seven Powers be enough to bring you success in your life. Implementing the Power of Belief will do you no good if you do not implement the Power of Action. The Power of Action alone is worthless without the Power of Mind.

Although the Seven Powers do not work independently of each other, together they can work wonders. And those powers are available to you at this very moment. Don't listen to the voices from your past that have told you that you are not worthy. Ignore the voices from the present that tell you that you will not succeed. They do not decide your future. You alone make that determination.

Before you lies a new future which you alone will write. Begin now to master the Seven Powers and build your success.

5

THE POWER OF CHOICE

Deep in the darkest dungeon of a vast castle you lie, watching the rats scurry across your dimly lighted cell floor. You have been buried here for so long now that you can't remember what the sky looks like or how the wind feels. Escape has proven impossible since the walls of your cell are carved from solid stone. Still, you have clawed at the stone until your hands bled, and then you clawed again.

Your best friends are hopelessness and despair. You haven't seen another living being for years. The only contact you have with the human race is your jailer, who comes once a day to give you your meager meal.

You have tried talking to him, but he never responds. Sometimes you would rather he curse you outright than continue the abhorrent silence you have so long endured.

"How long must I be imprisoned?" you cry, but no one answers. No one ever does.

One day, out of rage and frustration, you hurl your body against the solid iron door, heedless of the danger. To your surprise, the door moves just the smallest bit. Suddenly hope once again springs to life within your heart and you exert your full strength against the thick, iron door. Gradually the door opens, wider and wider, until you are able to squeeze through.

Silently and cautiously, you slip down the dungeon hallway and up a flight of stairs. After dozens more hallways and stairways, the passage abruptly terminates at a great door. There is light shining from under the door and voices come from within. There is no other way out, so cautiously, ever so cautiously, you open the door and step into a large room. The room is filled with people dressed in bright clothing and the air is filled with festivity.

All at once, the music stops and everyone turns toward you. Your heart stops as terror envelops you, but instead of alarm, there is curiosity on their faces. One of the people, an elderly gentleman, walks over to you and invites you to a rich table, laden with choice foods.

After you have eaten, the man looks at you and asks why he has never seen you before. You hesitate to answer because a misstep might land you once again in the prison. But the gentleman has a kindly air about him, so you gamble and say, "I have long been imprisoned in the dungeon of this castle and cruelly mistreated. It is only today that my jailer became careless and left my cell unlocked."

At this, the man becomes greatly disturbed and collapses into the nearest chair. "My good sir!" he exclaims. "Didn't you know? How long were you imprisoned?"

"Sir," you reply, "I have lost track of all time and have been imprisoned years beyond reckoning. What is it that I should have known?"

With shock written in every line of his face, the man

answers, "Didn't you know that the prison doors are never locked? You have always had the power to free yourself!"

Would you believe that you are, at this very moment, exactly where you have chosen to be in life? That, where you live, what job you have, your relationships or lack of them, the amount of money you have, every situation in your life, you have chosen to one degree or another? Either you have chosen those situations yourself or allowed others to choose them for you.

"No!" you protest. You are in this situation because misfortune has beset you, because people have treated you unfairly, because you were not born into privilege, wealth, and power. You didn't have the education you needed. You were tricked into marrying the wrong person. You didn't have the beauty, wit, or talent that you needed in order to be a success.

You say if you really had your choice, you would be wealthy, happy, and fulfilled, and yet you are not. Therefore, you reason, you could not possibly have chosen your present situation.

Certainly, there are many things that people cannot, and do not, choose. The loss of a loved one, a debilitating disease, a sudden injury, or a criminal attack are just a few things over which there is little or no control. But even in those situations you are not without choice. While it might be true that you cannot change those circumstances, you can choose your attitude, and thus, your response to them. Will you let the circumstances master your attitude, or will you choose in what manner you face them?

So, while granting a concession to the unforeseen calamities you experienced, the fact remains that everything else in your life you have chosen.

Why is it such a statement brings freedom to some people and anger to others? It is because to admit that one's life is largely the result of choice places the responsibility and the consequences of one's life squarely on the shoulders of every individual human being.

If your life really is a result of your own choice then you, and nobody else, is responsible for your present situation.

The Easiest Path

For just a moment, just for the sake of argument, accept the premise that one's life is the result of his own decision and choices. Supposing this were true, wouldn't everyone choose happiness instead of pain? If destiny is mostly a matter of choice, then why are so many people's lives filled with loneliness, frustration, poverty, and shame?

The reason is because man always takes the path of least moral resistance, usually with a bundle of rationalization tucked under each arm. Simply put, a great percentage of the time, man will take the easiest route in whatever decision he is asked to make. It is just easier to choose the less difficult road if it brings pleasure or delays pain.

Why go to college if you can get a good paying job now? Why get marriage counseling when divorce seems easier? Why discipline your children when they will be quiet if you just give them what they want?

Quite often the easiest choice is the decision that is based on an emotional bias, rather than intellectual reasoning. Take a moment and think about all the bad decisions you have made in your life. Think about the wrong turns, the bad relationships, the money mismanaged and misspent. Is it not true that the great majority of all the poor decisions that you made were based on emotion?

In such situations, people always declare they're following their heart, but if you look carefully, you'll see they're really being swept away by their emotions.

The young couple runs away together because of their infatuation, not because each has determined his or her partner has the qualifications to be a good mate. The middle-aged man gets a second mortgage on his house for a questionable investment, not because it is sound, but because he wants to get rich quickly. The family goes into debt to take a vacation, not because it was the smartest thing to do, but because they believed it would bring them pleasure.

The problem with such decisions is that they always produce consequences. When a person chooses poorly, he is, in effect, choosing the bad consequences that come bundled with his decision.

The young couple finds they lack the maturity for a long-term relationship. The middle-aged man now has two mortgages on his home rather than just one and is no closer to wealth. The family has to sacrifice in other areas because of their week of indulgence.

But, you ask, what if someone else made decisions that affected my destiny? To allow someone else to choose for you was a choice that you made. You found it easier to relinquish control than to accept responsibility for your own actions. Will you let them master your attitude, or will you choose in what manner you face them?

The one who doesn't believe he has chosen his lot in life is not recognizing that his choices and their consequences are one and the same. To choose a path is to choose its destination. The traveler cannot grumble about the destination if he is responsible for choosing the path.

Seizing Control

To be successful you must be the master of your emotions. Either you master your emotions or they will master you. There is no middle ground. You must learn to analyze decisions on a rational, and not emotional, basis. In doing so, you employ the limitless Power of Choice.

There are countless people in this world who were born into horrible situations and yet are tremendous successes. There are many stories of people who have been born into slavery but won their freedom. There are those born into the physical slavery of a debilitating physical affliction but have overcome and fought their way to success against all odds. There are those who have been beaten, imprisoned, starved, and ridiculed, who have refused to be deterred from their mission.

Such people have achieved success by choosing not to let their circumstances limit them. Many of them will tell you that the hardship and suffering they experienced only made them stronger. They chose to abandon fairy-tale thinking and employ the Seven Powers, rather than accept the lot which life handed them.

It's important to remember that everyone possesses the Seven Powers. If one person can achieve success another

To choose a path is to choose its destination. The traveler cannot grumble about the destination if he is responsible for choosing the path.

can also. All things being equal, the only difference between one person's life of tremendous success and another's of dismal failure is simply that each person made different choices. Each took a different path with far different outcomes. No life is written in stone and everyone possesses the Power of Choice.

Have you made mistakes that have had unpleasant circumstances? Do you groan under the weight of the consequences of such mistakes? Know then that the measure of an individual is not

> *All things being equal, the only difference between one person's life of tremendous success and another's of dismal failure is simply that each person made different choices.*

whether he ever makes mistakes, but what he does about the mistakes he makes. You now have the privilege and responsibility to decide.

Conclusion

You hold in your hand the power to direct your life wherever you desire. You have been told that life just happens to you and there is nothing you can do about it, but now you are armed with knowledge. Now you know better. Don't ever position of thinking life is an accident. Grasp the Power of Choice.

Choose to take a finance class. Choose to pay off your debt. Choose to take dancing lessons. Choose to ask the girl on a date. Choose to work on your marriage.

The story of your life is not complete, but one day it will be. When the story of your life is read, will the reader read about a person that feebly plodded on through life, not realizing the power at his disposal? Or will they read of a champion who unsheathed the Power of Choice, took life by the reins, and boldly made decisions that steered his life on the course he intended?

The choice is yours.

THE POWER OF VISION

$\mathfrak{I}$ t had been more than thirty years since the four friends had seen each other. As they sat around a table in the back of the same inn they had frequented in their youth, they exchanged an endless number of anecdotes from long ago. Peals of laughter escaped the corner table where they sat, and the other diners looked at them curiously. They didn't mind, though. This was a once-in-a-lifetime occurrence and each of the old friends cared nothing about the attention of the other people in the restaurant.

Although each of the four was very different from the others, they all had managed to remain fast friends through-out their childhood and adolescence. They had certainly had their disagreements, but being from a small village and being the same age, they always managed to resolve them, and were the best of friends until the day they graduated and went their separate ways.

John had been the school's star athlete, excelling prima-rily in running and wrestling. His good looks and charm made him a natural favorite and he had been the most popular boy in school. John's charisma and charm had won everybody he met, including his teachers, and it was a given that he would go far in life. Such capable and talented young men were in great demand in the king's court, and John rarely, if ever, worried about his future. John would just laugh, saying that life was good so why be concerned about tomorrow?

Phillip was the smart one of the group and had a great interest in chemistry and the sciences. He possessed a strong curiosity about what made things work and had spent hours mixing various plants and herbs together, attempting to create new medicines. Of course, he rarely had ever made less than one hundred percent on all his exams. Everyone in the village had excitedly speculated about what Phillip might become. With a mind such as his, they reasoned, the possibilities were limitless. That he would become a famous physician or serve as a medical advisor to the king was, in their minds, just a matter of time.

Nigel's parents would have preferred having him tutored at their estate, but he would have none of it. Instead, he insisted on attending school in the village with his friends, much to his mother's horror. It was true that he could be a bit spoiled at times, but it was no fault of his own, being the only child of doting parents with more money than sense. Nigel grew up not wanting for anything and always had the newest toys and clothes. He was mostly an average student and, if he did occasionally score poorly on an exam, no one seemed to mind. After all, Nigel's place in the world was considered to be guaranteed. His father was a wealthy merchant, and Nigel was sole heir of his entire fortune. Nigel was very well liked in school because, whatever his other faults, stinginess was not one of them. He had plenty of money and didn't mind spreading his wealth a bit. He enjoyed the attention that his generosity brought and found that his money easily bought him all the friends he could want.

William stood out least amongst his friends but was probably the oddest of them all. In fact, it was rather easy to overlook William altogether, in the company of his friends. He certainly wasn't as good-looking or as strong as John. Phillip was by far his intellectual superior and, being from a relatively poor family, it seemed William would never have the money that Nigel did. Most of the time William seemed bored and disinterested in school and almost everyone interpreted this as an ominous sign. As graduation loomed near, they repeatedly advised him to learn a craft or skill by which he could make a living.

What almost everybody overlooked about William was that he loved to read. He hungrily devoured book after book on almost any subject. Biographies were his favorite, although he liked history and fiction as well. He would spend hours reading after he finished his homework and sometimes would forgo playing in the yard in order to have more time for reading. He spent hours daydreaming about traveling to far away, exotic places, fighting battles of long ago, and engaging in daring adventures. In school, he found it difficult to focus on the monotonous drone of the teacher's lecture and wandered off in his mind to the wonderful places and things he had read about the night before.

Before long, the books that he had read began to fashion his young mind. He began to see the world as a larger place than his own village. He realized that an entire world existed beyond the borders of his small hamlet. He began to see the world with the eyes of some of the greatest writers and thinkers of the world. He unconsciously started to develop his imagination and to focus on the possibilities that his world had to offer. He began to have vision.

After the plates were cleared and most of the old stories had been recalled, the conversation inevitably began to turn toward what had happened since graduation. It was agreed that each would take turns telling his story, and they would start with John.

Everyone was curious about John because it was clear he was not the same young man of limitless possibilities he had once been. He was considerably overweight and bore years of hardship and trial in the lines of his face.

John looked down at his cup and fidgeted uncomfortably with his spoon.

"Well, I'm afraid my story is not much to tell," he began. "I busted up my knee pretty bad in a wrestling competition during my first year at the university. Right after that, I lost my scholarship on account of not being able to compete. The thing of it was, I might have been able to work my way back but, well, I started running around, having a good time in the local pubs, instead of working on getting better and, well, I kind of just never finished school."

His old friends offered their sympathies and assured him that such things could happen to anyone.

"Yeah," he said, shaking his head, "I guess so, but I knew other fellas that got hurt and worked their way back. I always regretted that I didn't do the same.

"I thought the thing to do would be to go get a job, but that didn't turn out to be as easy as I thought it would, either. Seemed like everybody wanted to talk to me about sports but nobody wanted to give me work. Every place I went, it was either I didn't have the experience or I didn't have the education. I finally wound up taking a job over at the mill and have been there ever since. It's amazing how everybody loves you when you're on top of your game, but you can't find friends that want to help you when you're down!" he said bitterly.

"I know just what you mean," said Nigel, shaking his head. "After my dad's business foundered, I couldn't pay anyone to speak to me... and I mean that both literally and figuratively!" he said laughing.

The group all chuckled and seemed to appreciate the opportunity to have another laugh. This part of their conversation was turning out to be more serious than any of them had anticipated.

"I guess you probably all know my story, or at least part of it," continued Nigel. "I know it's been told all over town. My father's health failed him just after we graduated. After he died, we found that his business was greatly in debt. After all the business was liquidated and all the bills were paid, there wasn't much money left. My mother's heart was broken and she wasn't long in following my father to the grave.

"As for me, I was able to complete college but certainly didn't break any academic records, unless you're talking about the ones for the worst students," he said wryly.

"Since then, I've invested in at least a dozen different businesses but none of them has ever panned out. It seems every time I invest, the value of the business plummets! To make ends meet, I got a job as a clerk at the local bank and have been working to keep my head above water ever since."

"I know just what you mean," said Phillip. "It seems I've been trying keep my head above water my whole life!"

This, of course, was scoffed at by the others at the table. After all, Phillip was a respected physician! What would he know of hardship?

"No, I'm serious," said Phillip, motioning the others quiet. "Since my family was not wealthy, I had to borrow a great deal of money to attend the university. When I finally got out of school, I had a mountain of debt. Then there were the start-up costs of my practice and many people are not able to pay my fees."

The others at the table still looked skeptical but were quieter now. They weren't used to hearing a physician speak this way. Weren't all physicians rich?

"The worst part," said Phillip, "is that I'm virtually a slave to my practice. When I'm not there, the money isn't coming in. As you know, I never married and have no social life whatsoever. This certainly isn't how I thought I'd wind up."

For a moment, everyone at the table was lost in his own thoughts and had nothing to say. Finally, John broke the silence. "Well, what about you, Will? Can you beat our sad stories or do I get the prize?"

William laughed and said, "Well, I don't know if I'll win the prize or not, John. I'll let all of you be the judge of that.

"When I graduated, I took a year off and saved some money for college. Since my parents weren't really in the position to help, I had to pay for college myself. When I finally did get to the university, I certainly had my work cut out for me. You might remember I wasn't the best student in school, but fortunately, in college, I got to select my own areas of study, and that helped hold my attention.

"After I received my degree, I was eager to conquer the world with my vast arsenal of book-knowledge," he laughed. "But as you can guess, it didn't really work that way.

"My first business failed within the first year and I lost everything I had put into it. I wound up owing thousands after my second business died and it took me a long time to dig myself out of that one.

"The good news was that, after having two businesses fail, I knew a little bit about what to do and what not to do. I started my third business, grew it over a period of fifteen years or so, and sold it a few years ago. I took some time off after that but got a little restless. Now, I advise the king on matters of commerce."

"Wow, Will," John said, "you're a lucky guy to have finally stumbled onto the right business!"

At this, William winced slightly and said, "Well, I'm not a big believer in Lady Luck, John. I've found she's a fickle mistress and can't be depended on when you need her most."

Intrigued, John leaned toward William and asked, "If that's so, why did you wind up being so successful and the rest of us are still a bunch of paupers?"

Everyone at the table chuckled, and Phillip laughingly declared he was of a different class of bum because he was a respected doctor.

William politely dodged John's question, saying he was the biggest pauper of all, reasoning that he came from the most humble beginnings. But the others at the table wouldn't let him off so easily.

"Seriously," said Nigel, "that's just what I mean. We all started in the same village, attended the same school, and you were the least well-off than any of us. How on earth did you do so well?"

William took a big breath and exhaled, saying, "My friends, that's quite a long story. I'm not sure you want to hear it."

"But you are one of the king's counselors!" Phillip said. "Why not let your friends benefit from some of that knowledge of yours? What one thing do you possess that made you successful that the rest of us lack?"

William looked around at his friends. His reluctance to speak was obvious. "Gentlemen, I would be the last person in the world to tell you that I'm successful and you're not. While it is true that I've been able to accomplish some of the things that I had hoped, I would like to think that each of you, at this very moment, are on your way to fulfilling your own amazing success stories. Also, I have to tell you, I don't think it's possible for one thing to make someone successful. Rather, I believe a number of things contribute toward the building of a success mentality.

"But if you are asking me if there is one element in my life that I've nurtured and developed that I see might be lacking in your own, that one thing would be vision."

"How do you mean, Will?" asked John. "You know that I wanted to be a great athlete. How did I lack vision?"

"Well, John, since you asked, I might suggest that you had the total package when we were growing up. You experienced some amazing, local, athletic success early in life, but it came too easily. You never learned to struggle through failure. Failure can be a great tutor and can strengthen you.

But, because success came so easily, you never developed your skills and honed your natural ability.

"But more important, in regard to vision, I believe you abandoned your vision of greatness too easily because you never had to fight for your success.

"I know, I know," William said, anticipating John's objection. "I know your injury hurt your chances of success in the world of sports, but you were capable of so much more than sports. Because of your natural athletic ability, you never developed your other strengths. In other words, you let your natural gifts limit your vision.

"It's like a weight lifter who focuses all his attention on upper-body strength but does nothing to build his leg muscles. His chest and abdomen look good but his legs aren't strong enough to take him very far."

As John sat and struggled with the meaning of William's words, Nigel spoke up, saying, "Would you say the same thing about me, William? I mean, I certainly had vision. I was once rich and I want to be rich again one day. Isn't that vision? Where would you say I went wrong?"

"Nigel," William answered, "you know that you were the one that everyone envied when we grew up, but thinking back, I guess you were the most handicapped, too.

"Think about it for a moment. You have spent most your adult life looking for the next big deal but have never found it. Have you ever wondered why that might be?

"I think part of it might be that you grew up trusting in the success of your father but never realized, nor developed, your own resources and strength. You assumed wealth and security would always be there, so you only thought about today.

You never looked at the possibilities of tomorrow. You never learned to recognize or create opportunity so, when the time came that you needed such skills, they simply weren't there."

"I think something like not looking toward tomorrow might have been my problem as well," said Phillip. "I mean, I gave attention to the responsibilities of tomorrow, but not to my dreams. What do you think, William?"

"I think you're right," William replied. "You knew what you wanted from an early age but let your vision get derailed by life's distractions. I know you once desired to be a famous physician or serve as a medical advisor to the king. I know you desired to help people by discovering new cures and treatments for disease, but now you are burdened with a heavy workload and a mountain of debt.

"Think of it this way: You started on the journey, arranged the proper transportation, and bought the ticket, but forgot where you wanted to go. You were distracted with loading your luggage, finding your seat, and making your connections. Now you are at a destination at which you never intended to be."

John shook his head and said, "I always thought I knew what having vision was, but maybe I've been way off the mark."

Phillip motioned to the innkeeper to fill his cup, took a sip, and voiced his agreement. "William, you have three old friends here that need your help, and we're not letting you out of here until you teach us something about vision!"

The first thing you have to understand about vision is that it is, as the word implies, seeing—yes, seeing your objective, but also seeing your purpose, your desire, and your tomorrow. Visionaries always see their objective completed before it begins. They envision their ideas so clearly that they can imagine the way the end-result looks, smells, and feels. Not only do they imagine the idea completed, but more important, they also imagine what reaching that goal will mean to them.

> *Visionaries always see their objective completed before it begins.*

The real estate developer not only imagines the building completed; he sees himself enjoying the profits he will realize as the result of the project. A mother not only sees her children being obedient; she sees her children walking through life successfully.

Not only do visionaries see what they want; they know why they want it. This causes the visionary to have a burning passion for his project. The visionary is consumed with possibility. So much so that, to him, it seems a small step from the possible to the probable. When others around him aren't sure if it will work, he knows it will. When others falter, his step is sure.

Another major element of vision is focus. Focus is the lens through which the images of objective, purpose, desire, and tomorrow are channeled. It is a magnifying glass held over a thin piece of paper. Without the glass, the sun's rays are indeed powerful, but not enough to have any immediate effect. When intensified through the magnifying glass, though, the sun's heat will produce a very definite effect on the paper.

The purpose of focus is to concentrate energy and effort in one specific direction for maximum effectiveness. Without focus, your vision is distracted and intermittent; your efforts scattered and misdirected.

The visionary's focus is directed and intensified by the desire produced by knowing and visualizing his objective. He knows it is impossible to focus if he is unsure of his target.

People with vision have an edge on their competition because, unlike just about everybody else, they know where they want to go, what they want, and why they want to get there.

Their reason to succeed is never far from their conscious thought because they have built that reason upon the deepest foundations of their being.

Discovering Your Purpose

You have a purpose for which you were placed in this world.

You were meant for more than income production. Your life has greater value than just paying bills. It has greater value than just making sure all your creditors are happy and that you have enough for one more day.

Do you know your purpose? Do you know the reason that you have been placed on this planet? Most people don't and never will.

If a goal is your destination, and a plan is the map that will lead you there, then purpose is the reason you are taking the journey in the first place. Knowing your purpose is crucial when making your goals and building your plan.

Not paying attention to your purpose is not paying attention to your destination. If you don't know why you want to go someplace, then you have greatly increased your chances of not liking it once you arrive.

For example, it could prove disastrous if a man wanted to be a successful attorney but didn't spend time clarifying why he wanted to become one. Perhaps his real

> *If a goal is your destination, and a plan is the map that will lead you there, then purpose is the reason you are taking the journey.*

desire was to spend time with his family and have enough money to be able to give to charitable causes. Maybe he reasoned he would be able to do these things if he had enough money and thought the way to have enough money would be to engage in a well-paying job. But what if he didn't enjoy that job and found it constraining and suffocating? What if he underestimated the number of hours he needed to spend in order to get to the level where he had free time? In that case, he would find it extremely frustrating to spend his life immersed in such a profession and would definitely not be fulfilling his purpose, no matter how much money he made.

If, on the other hand, a woman found fulfillment as an accountant by helping people bring order to the chaos of their financial records, then she might be fulfilling her purpose. Even though she would certainly experience difficult times in her profession, knowing her purpose would guide her toward achieving success.

Of course, some people feel that, in order to fulfill their purpose in life, they must choose a profession which is traditionally not known for its abundance in compensation, such as a policeman, teacher, or missionary. Such people, whether they realize it or not, are essentially trading the chance of financial gain for the opportunity of fulfilling their purpose. They have chosen their desire to help people over their desire to be financially well-off.

That is not to say that fulfilling one's purpose and becoming wealthy are mutually exclusive! There is nothing wrong in and of itself with being rich. There is something wrong with desiring nothing else in life other than to consume.

When contemplating your purpose, you must ask yourself what you want to contribute to this world. In this life, you are either contributing something of value to the world or you are taking something away. There is no middle ground. It is, however, quite possible to prosper while you contribute to this world. Many musicians, architects, contractors, artists, entrepreneurs, doctors, writers, athletes, and others have grown wealthy while giving their time and talents in their unique ways.

When searching for your purpose, the most important question to ask yourself is, why are you here? Why are you on planet Earth? What are you here to do? What are you here to be?

Why you are here is one of the biggest questions you will ever have to answer and, although other people can offer assistance and guidance, no one can, or should, answer that question for you.

In your quest to answer this question, you will have to examine your life philosophy (*Who am I? Where do I come from? What do I believe about God?*) or develop your philosophy, if you don't already have one. The journey to discovering your purpose is almost as important as knowing what your purpose is, because it will cause you to reach deeper within and look closer at yourself than you ever have before. It will change the person that you are by digging a deeper foundation for the person you are to become.

Be careful to realize that the question of one's purpose cannot, and will not, be answered overnight, in a few weeks, or even a few months. Avoid accepting the first idea that pops into your head. Also avoid looking for a grandiose reason such as being placed here to bring enlightenment to the world or a flimsy reason such as being placed here to be the best singer.

For most people, the answer is much simpler and much more profound.

All of your plans, every decision you make, every opportunity you evaluate, will be subject to this one, overriding paradigm. If, as time goes by, you find that you have to alter your perception of what your purpose is, don't worry. It is usually a sign of growth. Very few people start with one idea of their purpose and end with the same. Embrace, rather than reject, the evolution of your concept of your purpose.

Determining Your Desires

After you have determined your purpose, you must determine your desires. What is it that you want out of life? Be honest. Forget right and wrong answers. So often people answer this question with what they think sounds best or what they feel they should answer or even what they think other people would want them to answer.

The question is, what do you want? Do you want children? Then say so. Do you want to be rich? Then be honest with yourself, but be careful to be specific. Instead of saying you want to be rich, define what it is you want.

- Not, "I want to be rich," but, "I want to retire when I'm _____ years old with a monthly income of $_____."
- Not, "I want a wife," but, "I want a faithful companion and soulmate with whom I can share my life."
- Not, "I want to help people," but, "I want to help inner-city children by teaching them to read."

It truly is an amazing fact that most people do not know what they want. The world is filled with fairy-tale thinkers who are fifty- or sixty-years old who still don't know what they want out of life—people who are caught in an endless pattern of indecision simply because they have never engaged in the discipline of focused thought on the subject.

When you start to think about what you want, it is imperative that you write it down. But write it down in pencil. As you get older, what you want changes. Even so, don't let that keep you from writing down what you want now. Remember, success is not a destination or a one-time event. It is an evolution and development.

As you begin the process of writing down your desires, you will find you have different desires for different areas of your life—some spiritual, some financial, some family-oriented, and some physical. You will want to make different

*Vision is the ability to see
your purpose, your desire,
and your tomorrow.*

lists for each of these categories and refer to them often. They will serve as great motivation to you as you work toward them.

Don't let the fact that you don't know how to achieve these desires prohibit you from writing them down. How to achieve them is a job for the Power of Mind and it is not necessary for you to think about that now. If you happen to think of a couple of great ideas about how they might be accomplished, then by all means, write them down. But the purpose of this task is not to create the means to get you there, but to help you decide where "there" is.

Determining your desires is the selection of the mission on which you will soon embark. How can you go on a mission without knowing where you want to go? And yet, every day, millions of people on this planet do so without even wondering where the road leads.

Your purpose will send you on the mission, but your desire will direct and drive you. Your desires are not meant to be your slave master, relentlessly driving you onward toward achievement, but rather your motivation and encouragement, accompanying you as you travel.

Discerning Your Tomorrow

What would you give to be able to look into the future? How much would you pay to know what your life will be like in five years? What would you do to be able to know how much you will be making, where you will be working, and where you will live one or five years from now? Do you think that information might be helpful in making decisions today? Would that information be valuable to you?

To a large degree, almost everybody has that ability at this very instant. The irony is that, although most people would agree that such an ability would be valuable and useful, they will never access that power!

Every year mediums and spiritualists rake in untold amounts of money from people desperate to know what lies ahead in their future—people infected with fairy-tale thinking who believe that someone can tell them some vital piece of information that will give them power. How sad!

How sad, especially when they hold that power themselves.

So, how does one look into one's future? By simply looking at where he is today and tracing the direction he is heading. Sure, it sounds pretty simplistic, but take just a moment and think about it.

When someone is walking down the street, it doesn't take any genius to make a pretty good guess at where the person will be in another five, ten, or fifteen steps. Of course, he could turn suddenly in to a coffee shop or down an alley, but even those occurrences can be predicted somewhat by the inclination of his body or the consistency of his gait.

Now, taking the example a bit further, suppose you want to know where he will be at 7:00 p.m. a month from now. That will require a good bit more investigation on your part. You might follow him for several weeks to study his habits and learn that on this day of the week, he always stays late at the office. Now you can make an educated guess as to where he will be at 7:00 p.m. in another month.

Now suppose you applied that same reasoning to your own life. After all, no one knows more about your activities than you. Based on how you are spending your time daily and barring the unforeseen, you should have a good idea of where you will be one month, one year, or even five years from now. Do you like what you see?

Now factor in various unexpected calamities and look at what your life might be like. Think about an unexpected injury or about losing your job. How do you like that picture?

Someone accessing the Seven Powers can use this information to strengthen his position and guard against hardship. When he does, people around him nod their heads and whisper in reverential tones about how much foresight this individual had to anticipate such a thing and to prepare for it.

Surprisingly, fairy-tale thinkers constantly use this technique. But instead of factoring the unexpected calamity, they include the unexpected windfall and plan (or more accurately, don't plan) accordingly. They think something wonderful is going to happen, never bothering to pay attention to their current heading, and are surprised when they find themselves ten years into the future in the same old dead-end job or relationship.

Conclusion

Vision is not a gift. It is not a talent. It is a learned skill that is available to everyone. It is the focus of clearly seeing your purpose, your desire, and your tomorrow.

Those who have vision posses a power that others do not. They are guided by an objective which they see clearly and vividly, like a shining tower in the distance. Since they have such a clear picture of where they want to go and why they are going, when they do encounter obstacles, they view them differently than most people. Instead of thinking of them as obstructions barring their way to success, people with vision see them as merely one more thing that must be checked off on their to-do list. They expect difficulty and therefore are not deterred or defeated when they encounter it.

No one can see the future with one-hundred-percent accuracy, but developing the skill of vision will grant you a power beyond that of most people who walk the earth.

THE POWER OF MIND

You are the ruler of a country that is at war against a ruthless enemy. Daily your enemy assails your country's borders in a multitude of merciless, unrelenting attacks. This war has continued for a number of years and analysis indicates that you are certainly losing. The brief victories you have experienced are quickly forgotten in the inevitable, subsequent defeats. Your soldiers are weary, your supplies are nearly depleted, and your morale is low. Now it seems nothing less than a miracle will save you from a cruel enemy that seeks to kill you, enslave your people, and possess your land.

As you sit in your throne room, contemplating surrender, a sudden commotion in the outer hall pierces the quiet. Voices are raised. People are shouting. Could your enemy have finally breached your defenses and now be at your gates?

A courier appears at the door and requests permission to approach the throne. After being granted permission, he approaches and exclaims, "Your Highness, a great discovery has been made!"

The courier goes on to explain that in a distant province, a wondrous building has been excavated which contains many weapons that appear to have strength beyond any you now possess. This arsenal holds a vast array of arms, all of cunning and deadly design. You learn that the operation of many of the weapons is not presently understood, but your scientists are making rapid progress in unlocking their secrets.

It appears that no one had any knowledge or memory of such an arsenal, and it is a wonder that it has never been discovered. One would think it had been preserved for a time of dire need, such as the one in which you now find yourself.

For the first time since the war began, you actually have an excellent chance of defeating your enemy and bringing peace back to your land. Your heart soars. You feel like dancing for joy. At last, an answer to the dilemma that almost destroyed everything you hold dear!

What would such an answer be worth to you? What price would you pay to find such an arsenal?

Think about the battles you now fight. The battle against poverty. The battle against loneliness. The battle against disability. The battle against monotony and despair.

What if you were to find that you were already in possession of a marvelous arsenal that contains all the weapons you need to defeat your enemy? What would that be worth to you?

You are now in possession of such an arsenal. Within your mind you have all the weapons you need to defeat any enemy that now assails you. You might not be aware of the full power of this arsenal, or have mastered the use of its many weapons, but with exploration and examination, you will find the measure of its worth. When you learn to unleash the Power of Mind, you have the ability to actually alter reality—your reality. You can change your job, the amount of money you have, your love life, the way people perceive you, and the way you perceive people. Your mind holds the key to changing your life.

Your Creativity Weapon

Within your mind you hold the power of creativity. Look around you. Everything you see began as an idea. More important, and more to the point, everything you see began as someone's idea. Someone had an idea and implemented it. All the things you see in front of you began as only a germ of thought in someone's mind. Now think of the wealth represented by all the manufactured products you see. Just think of it! Somebody had an idea and turned it into income. He converted a mere thought into a tangible object that, in turn, produced money. In effect, he changed reality. Maybe just the smallest bit, but the world is now changed because of one person's idea.

What about you? What about your ideas? Are you cultivating your ideas? Are you giving them life by exploring their possibilities?

Of course, not all ideas will be, or should be, brought to completion. But all ideas are stepping stones. Even a bad idea, if cultivated and developed, can serve to take you to the next, better idea. But if you are in the habit of immediately dismissing your ideas, you will never get to the better ones. If you continually reject your ideas, after a while, they will cease altogether because you will develop the habit of ignoring them.

Perhaps you learned to dismiss and reject your ideas long ago. Why? Who told you that your ideas were worthless?

Did you lose faith in the validity and strength of your ideas at school, or was it a parent who told you that your ideas were foolish? Whatever the source, you have bought a lie. Maybe your ideas weren't the most original or the cleverest at the time, but they still had value.

Have you ever had a garden? Suppose you planted some vegetable seeds. You watered them for a week or so and then watched the tiny sprouts shooting from the ground. After a couple more weeks you saw the small plants that your seeds had become, but instead of excitement, you felt anger. In a fit of rage you went out into the garden and pulled every plant up and swore that you would never garden again. After all, it had been three weeks since you had planted! Why hadn't you already harvested bushels of vegetables?

Almost any gardener will tell you that it is ridiculous to expect most plants to produce after only three weeks. No, it takes time, just as ideas do. You can't expect the first appearance of an idea to be the best. It's just not practical. Whoever told you your ideas lacked merit lacked the vision to see those ideas coming to maturity over a period of time.

In addition to producing ideas, you should also develop the discipline of using your creativity to solve problems. Do you remember taking multiple-choice quizzes in school? You were given an option of choosing the answers A, B, C, or D. But consider this—what if the A, B, C, or D answers weren't the best options? On the tests you were given in school, the answers most likely were the best options, but real life rarely operates in the same manner.

You are told by a store clerk that you can either swap your merchandise for another item or get store credit. You are handed a menu with a limited selection as you are told to sit at a table near the noisy kitchen.

Creative problem solvers always look for Option X. If the A, B, C, and D options don't suit them, they look for the invisible option that will. They believe that somewhere on the quiz lies an invisible answer—one that isn't readily obvious but that will benefit the other party involved in the transaction, as well as benefiting them-selves. They have trained themselves

> *Creative problem solvers always look for Option X.*

to stop, examine the options before them, and explore additional possibilities. Sometimes it happens that the A, B, C, or D option really is the best choice, but creative problem solvers never assume that it is.

Creative problem solvers firmly believe that:

1] There is ALWAYS another way to do it, and

2] Every problem has a solution.

In creative problem solving, it is essential to accept and believe these two postulates, because if you don't believe in the existence of something, you won't look for it.

Have you ever heard anyone say, "That's the way we've always done it, and it's always worked before," or, "It won't work that way. We tried it that way and it didn't work"? People in the habit of such thinking limit their creative resources and thus, their options for solutions and success, because they already have made up their minds. Because their minds are made up, they are satisfied to look no further.

Your Imagination Weapon

You also hold within your mind the power of imagination. Before you can ever transition into anything other than what you are now, you must conceive it first. Fairytale thinkers believe that merely conceiving the image of being rich and famous will somehow make them so. People who utilize the Power of Mind use their imagination as a blueprint for their lives and then seek ways to build their picture.

Think for a moment. Imagine the sort of person you would like to be. Be specific. Don't think in terms such as, "I want to help people." Help them by doing what? Think of the people whom you admire. What about them do you admire? Now, using those various components from those different people, build the person you would like to be. How much money would this person have? Remember not to reply in abstract answers. Exactly how much money would this person have? How much money do you need? How would this person spend his time? How is this person perceived by other people? Why? Is this person a spiritual person?

If the answer to these questions results in a "filthy rich and lazy" picture, you need to start over. If the sum of your aspirations is just to consume and not contribute, then you need to reexamine your purpose and start again.

When you draw this picture in your mind, remember to draw it in pencil, not ink. You will need to adjust this picture many times. As you grow and explore new possibilities, you will discover that many of your presuppositions were incorrect. For example, many people believe that all people who earn a lot of money have more free time. This is not necessarily so. Or, you might also discover that you have set your sights too low—that you are capable of so much more than you first imagined. It's perfectly acceptable to redraw your picture many times.

It is essential that you build a picture of the person that you desire to one day become so that you have a visual goal. You must have a clear target, or your efforts and energy will be wasted in running in the wrong direction. You will encounter many opportunities along your path. How will you know which to take? When you clearly visualize your mental goal, you need only that picture in order to see if an opportunity is something you need to pursue or merely a distraction from your ultimate goal. Will this opportunity take you toward being the person you would like to be, or will it waste years of your life?

Your Planning Weapon

Once you build your picture, it is time to begin employing one of the chief, and least-used, powers of the mind. The art of planning is your secret weapon.

Most of the people around you just let life happen to them. They go through a maze of circumstances and react to each of them in turn, but rarely ever construct their lives so that they are pointed in a specific direction. In short, they don't have a plan.

How many examples of this do you see daily? An older man's health fails and he can no longer work. A young, single woman finds herself pregnant without the means to support her baby. A couple buys new furniture on credit but doesn't have the income to pay for it. A man or woman dates someone for years who has made no declaration of a permanent relationship.

So what is a plan? A plan is simply a map to take you from where you are now to where you want to be. Imagine that you want to go to another city. Would you just start walking in a direction and hope it was the right one? No, you would study a map and plot a course that led to your destination.

Similarly, when you make your plan, you will need to recall your mental picture and then begin seeking the steps needed to take you there. Will you need more education? Will you need financing? Will you need dance or music lessons? Will you need counsel?

Be sure not to wait for the perfect plan. It doesn't exist. The saying "better an imperfect plan today, than a perfect plan tomorrow" is absolutely true. Therefore, it is important that the plan you choose be malleable.

If, after giving your plan a fair trail, you find that it is not working, change the plan or get another one! Don't become emotionally attached to it. A plan is only a road map. It is not the destination. It is not the vehicle that will get you there. It is only a guide, and if your guide isn't taking you where you want to go, fire him and get another one!

But what about persistence? Isn't it important to persist? Certainly, but you should be persistent in the pursuit of your goal, not in adherence to your plan. They are not the same thing.

As important as the plan itself is the action of writing it down. If your plan isn't written down, then you don't have a plan; you have an idea. A written plan is there to guide you, to show you your progress, to let you know what elements of your strategy are working and which ones need to be modified.

Begin with where you are now and write down the steps you need to take you where you want to go. (If you are not sure what those are, then you will need to do some research.) Make the steps as small and detailed as possible so you have a clear idea of what tasks you

> *If your plan isn't written down, then you don't have a plan; you have an idea.*

must perform. Making the steps small also allows you to clearly mark your progress as you edge your way toward you dream.

Of course, there will be times you will have to improvise. Sometimes you will unexpectedly come upon a closed road and will have to take a detour. Having a written plan will allow you to take such detours and still find your way back to your original course.

The principle benefit of writing down your plan is that you are no longer attempting to achieve the impossible or chase a dream. Instead, you are checking off a to-do list that just happens to take you to success.

Think of writing down your plan as the first step of transforming your nontangible idea into a tangible reality. When you do so, you are literally changing one form of energy into another and, in doing so, are accomplishing more with your ideas than most people ever will.

Maintaining Your Arsenal

In utilizing the Power of Mind, it is of utmost importance that you make it your goal to constantly, consistently feed your mind. The key difference between someone who is successful and someone who is not is the way each of them thinks. If you are to fulfill your goals and dreams, you must be strengthening your mind. You must focus on keeping your mind in top condition.

How ridiculous would it be for an athlete to expect to win a race if he never conditioned his body, if he never gave his body the right foods, if he never exercised? Not only would he certainly not win, he could seriously injure himself by living a life of leisure and then subjecting his body to sudden exertion.

Your mind must also be trained because your intellect will atrophy if left unexercised. How ridiculous would it be for anyone to expect to succeed if he never conditioned his mind? Much financial and emotional injury is incurred by uninformed and uneducated individuals who launch into endeavors they are not sufficiently prepared to undertake.

By far, the best technique to strengthen your mind is reading. Reading engages your mind as no other medium does. When you read, you are employing your whole mind—your intellect, imagination, and creativity.

But not all reading is of the same value. Be careful of mental junk food—material you chew and digest but that has no real nutritional value. Some reading is meant purely for entertainment; other books and articles are written to inform; others to inspire. Be careful to make sure you have a well-balanced reading diet. It is true in regard to your body and it is true in regard to your mind: You are what you eat.

The key difference between someone who is successful and someone who is not is the way each of them thinks.

But no one book will change your life forever. It is important not only to read, but to keep reading. Think of books as the training wheels of the mind. Just as training wheels help the young bicyclist keep his balance until he can master the skills necessary to ride, so must your mind be guided as it learns to travel in new directions.

As you begin to replace the old thought patterns with the new, you will find your mind continuously reverting to the old way of thinking. You will automatically lapse into the old thought habits because, even though they have not served you well in the past, they are familiar and comfortable. Guard against this tendency by not reading just one book on a given topic, but several over a long period of time, until the new way of thinking is more comfortable than the old; until you own the new concepts and find they are thoroughly a part of you.

Another valuable technique in expanding your thinking is to associate with people that challenge you. Most people tend to only associate with like-minded people because they find it comfortable. But if you intend to live a successful life, you must make it a habit to associate with successful people. If it is true that the key difference between the successful and the unsuccessful is the way that each thinks, then you must learn to think as successful people do.

Do you know anyone that is more successful than you are? He may have a better marriage, his children may be better behaved, he may be better at his job, or he may have more money. If you do know such a person, make a point of spending time with him. Ask him if he would be willing to allow you to learn from him in the manner of an apprentice. Most people would be flattered at such a request, if you make it clear that you do not intend to monopolize their time.

Observe how he manages problems and compare your observations with the way you would react in a similar situation. How is he thinking differently? How does he spend his time every day? Ask him questions and take notes of his answers.

It is vital that you write down what you learn because you will not likely remember it if you do not. One of the characteristics of the unsuccessful is that they rarely, if ever, take notes. They say they would feel foolish doing so or they claim there is no reason to since they believe they will remember without writing anything down.

Another powerful method of maintaining and improving the Power of Mind is to develop the ability to reason—the ability to discern truth by an if/then process using only logic. The ability to reason is far and away more valuable than a traditional education alone. A formal education is wonderful to have, but is no guarantee that the student will learn to think and reason for himself. The world is full of educated fools.

Most people rarely develop the capacity to reason because of the human tendency to take the path of least resistance. Even with the educated, the intellect will almost always follow emotional bias rather than rational. People will choose what feels or seems best, rather than what makes the most intellectual sense.

It is just human nature to hear an opinion, agree with it, and count it as original thought. Someone will hear an argument, think it sounds reasonable, and accept it as his own, without ever questioning either the source or the logic. Much, much folly is perpetuated by this weakness.

To become and remain successful, you will need to cultivate a mental posture of reason. Learn to question, but don't fall into the trap of skepticism. There are many skeptical people in the world that doubt everything. But they simply are in the habit of being negative and are not exercising their intellect.

If you aspire to master the ability to reason, you must learn to evaluate the information you receive. What was the source of the information? Was the source biased in any way? Is the information subjective or objective? Is there an opposing viewpoint?

Never believe something just because you heard it, read it in a book, or heard a celebrity say it. Always verify. Always authenticate. Everyone has a bias. Just because someone is sincere doesn't mean he is right. Learn to make up your own mind, leaving ample room for adjustment.

Conclusion

Now that you are aware of your vast arsenal and have become familiar with the various weapons at your disposal, your enemies should no longer intimidate you. But make no mistake; you will most definitely still have to fight. You will have to master the weapons in your arsenal and use them to assail your enemies.

Do not allow your enemies to go unchallenged. Do not feebly submit to being a slave of loneliness, fear, poverty, boredom, or depression. Now is the time to draw your sword, to bend your bow, to flex your muscle, and stretch out your hand against your enemies. No one will do it for you. Nor does anyone need to, because you already have everything you need.

You have the Power of Mind.

THE POWER OF ACTION

𝕿 he day of the big game has finally arrived and your small village buzzes with anticipation! The excitement has been building around this match for as long as anyone can remember. It's the home team against its arch rival in a winner take all, do-or-die match! The championship team will win the honor of being received at the palace by none other than the king himself. It is the first time your village has ever been this close to fame and honor. No one in your small hamlet is left untouched by what this victory might mean in recognition and pride to the small community.

The home team has better talent than ever before. Everyone on the team is trained and strong. Nothing can stop them. Sure, there will be a struggle, but in the end, they are sure to win.

As the day begins to grow warm, the coach leads the team out onto the field. The crowd leaps to its feet and roars in support of the team. The team looks toned and confident. In front of the team runs the star player. He towers above the other players and his body is the picture of strength and agility.

As the other team is led onto the field, it seems as though there must be some sort of mistake. Can this be the opponent?

Can this be the arch rival of which so much has been made? Although their aggressiveness cannot be mistaken, the players look to be no match for the home team. As they run onto the field, their uniforms hang limply from their lean frames and they seem to possess none of the raw power and talent that your team has so much in abundance.

As the players run onto the field to begin the game, you notice your star player is sitting on the beach. Now, why would that be, you wonder. The coach is a wizened veteran of the game and must have some secret strategy.

The game begins and the visiting team soon takes the lead. No matter, though. There is plenty of time left in the game. But as the game progresses, you notice many of your players are starting to grow weary, and the star player is still not in the game. Why wouldn't the coach send him in?

Now the game is nearing completion. Your team has fought bravely and has struggled valiantly against a foe who has manifested every appearance of cheating. Many in the crowd have shouted, "Unfair! Unfair!" but their cries have seemed to do no good. The referees are deaf to their shouts and the game mercilessly continues.

But all hope is not lost! If the coach would send in the star player, your team might still be able to catch up. The coach finally looks over at the star as he sits on the bench. The coach finally motions for him to go into the game. The crowd, anxiously awaiting this signal, erupts in cheers! But what is happening? Could it be? In answer to the coach's signal, the star player firmly shakes his head. He is refusing to go into the game!

Instead, the star player cleans the game equipment. He cleans his shoes. He straightens his uniform, but he will not get into the game.

Inevitably, the clock runs out. Impossibly, the home team has suffered an overwhelming, humiliating defeat. As the buzzer sounds, signaling the game's end, the star player gets up from the bench and lopes back to the clubhouse. As the other players limp back toward the locker room, questions fill the minds of the fans. Why didn't the star play in the game? Was he afraid? Was he dishonest? Why did he sit on the bench when he was so perfectly fitted to be on the field?

Why are you sitting on the bench? Why aren't you in the game? Are you afraid? Have you been deceived? Are you being completely honest with yourself? There is one game. There is one chance. There is one life you have been given and there are no dress rehearsals.

It does not matter if a star player possesses natural talent, ability, and skill if he is not in the game. Remember that this book is your sign. It is your wake-up call. It is your signal to begin.

It is now time to employ the Power of Action and get into the game.

Many people spend their whole lives waiting for their ship to come in. How many times have you heard that expression or one like it?

"When my ship comes in, I'll buy a house."

"When my ship comes in, I'll travel all around the world."

"When my ship comes in, I'm going to find the right girl and settle down."

"When our ship comes in, we're going to start a family."

Too many people live their lives based on the fairy-tale notion that their ship will one day arrive. As if the only question were when the ship would arrive, not if it would arrive at all, they wait, doing little or nothing but marking time their whole lives.

But there is another alternative for the one who gets tired of waiting, and that option is to grab a hammer! That's right. Instead of waiting for your ship to come in, grab a hammer and build a boat. Why not take a chance and start doing something? Why not start working on a plan to take you to your destination? If, by some miracle, your ship does somehow come in after you build your boat, then you will have both the ship and a boat. If your ship never arrives, then you have a boat and won't get surprised by any unexpected floods.

Waiting for a ship to arrive one day is an extremely poor strategy, but for countless people, it is their primary plan. Because of their dependency on this strategy, they strenuously object to building their own boat.

"I can't start a business. I don't have the money!"

"I'll probably never find a mate. It just doesn't seem to be in the stars."

"I hate my job, but it's a paycheck and my children are depending on me."

The person who is determined to build his own boat has a completely different attitude. He goes and finds the money to start the business. He seeks to improve himself, believing

*Instead of waiting for your ship
to come in, grab a hammer
and build a boat.*

that water seeks its own level, and realizes that if he wants a good life partner, he must first be a good prospective life partner. He realizes that job security is an illusion and the biggest rewards in life are not found sitting on the bench, but getting into the game.

Talent Versus Skill

The world contains countless talented people who go through their entire lives warming the bench; they are some of the smartest, the strongest, the quickest, the most talented, and the most beautiful. But most of these people lack the one thing they need most in order to gain success. They lack application.

They have talent but have never applied themselves. Are you one of these people? Did good grades come easily to you? Did people think you were nice-looking? Did everyone think you had natural ability in music and were sure to go far?

What if you are on the other end of the spectrum? What if you were one of those who were overlooked because you didn't appear to have any marks of success? Did that keep you from trying? Did you come to believe that you didn't have a chance at success because you didn't possess natural ability or talent?

Understand this: Skill, bought by discipline and hard work, always triumphs over undeveloped, natural talent.

The greatest mistake most talented people make is that, being insufficiently challenged, they fail to gain the training they need to hone and perfect their natural talent. Since a small measure of success has come easily to them, they are cursed with the notion that their talent alone will always be enough. It rarely is.

Those who begin with little talent, though, and purchase their skill through long hours of study, labor, and self-deprivation, will in the end often surpass the ability of the naturally talented and see greater success because of it.

Working Harder

There is another type of individual who is already working hard but feels the answer to life's problems is working a little bit harder. He wants to be in the game all the time. He realizes that the balance of success and failure lies in every play and feels he needs to be "on call" virtually all the time. He is deceived into thinking that if he just works

> *The greatest mistake most talented people make is that, being insufficiently challenged, they fail to gain the training they need to hone and perfect their natural talent.*

a little harder, everything will work out. If he just gets an additional job or works an extra shift, then he can make ends meet.

The wise coach will rotate his players and not overuse his key athletes. You are that coach and your time, strength, and efforts are your key players. You must budget these assets through the game of life. If you overexert yourself in pursuit of a goal, you are not likely to finish the game.

Do not make the mistake of the young who believe they are immortal. You will not always have the strength you have today. There will be increasing demands on your time. More and more will be demanded of your mind and emotions.

The answer is to concentrate on finding ways of working smarter, not harder. As you implement the Power of Action, remember to utilize the Power of Mind. Focus your mind on solving your problem not by increasing activity, but by concentrating that activity through the implementation of your plan.

Your plan should take into consideration your age, health, and stamina; not only at present, but also throughout the lifespan of the plan.

Conclusion

If you are now sitting on the bench, the question you must ask yourself is, how long are you willing to accept an unbearable situation, day in and day out? Are you watching a losing game? Are you tired of being poor or lonely? Are you tired of being treated poorly? Do you hate your job, lifestyle, or where you live? If so, get into the game! Pick up a hammer! Dare to do!

This is the sign you have been waiting for.

Begin!

THE POWER OF FAILURE

There once lived a woman named Mary who made no mistakes—at least she liked to think so. She prided herself in the wisdom she practiced in making decisions.

Mary's motto was "better safe than sorry" and she had long since subconsciously adopted this as her life philosophy. Safety was her god. Security was her idol and daily she sacrificed her life on the altar of the mundane and worshipped in the temple of mediocrity.

Mary was the smartest person she knew. In her mind, she had done everything right. She had a good job where she was a model employee. She wasn't married, although she hoped that she one day would be, when Mr. Right finally came along.

She lived in a quiet neighborhood in a modest home. She attended the same school that her parents did and lived in the same area in which she was born.

Mary had a sister named Susan who was her opposite in every way. If there was a risk to be taken, Susan launched ahead. If there was a challenge that presented itself, Susan readily accepted. Mary always looked at Susan's activities with extreme disapproval and justified that disapproval by noting the many failures and disappoint-ments Susan suffered.

It was true that Susan had indeed been the recipient of many heartaches and setbacks. As a child, the local nurses and doctors all knew Susan by name, and her father joked that he paid for the hospital's new wing.

She was not the best of students because she had no fear in trying new ways of doing things. She found that most of her teachers were not truly interested in her really learning anyway. Most of the time, they just wanted her to obediently memorize countless facts, figures, names, and dates, and then mechanically repeat those facts, figures, names, and dates back to them on an endless number of exams. Her teachers called this teaching.

As a young woman, Susan worked a multitude of jobs and changed schools several times. Susan always sought adventure and knowledge, but Mary just saw her as reckless and fickle.

Many years passed and Susan became self-employed in the small town in which she and Mary lived. Mary, who worked at a government job, felt Susan's occupation was risky and hazardous. She constantly implored Susan to come to her senses and get a "good" job, which she defined as one like her own.

Susan had indeed failed at several businesses, but always found the resources to keep trying. She maintained that failure was just part of the process and seemed not as both-ered as Mary thought she ought to be. Mary interpreted Susan's tenacity only as folly. Why take the risk of self-em-ployment when nice, safe jobs were available for those who could pass the exams?

Before too long, there began to be ugly rumors in their town about business closings and layoffs. Soon, long lines began to form at the soup kitchens. More and more people were losing their jobs, but Mary wasn't worried in the least. After all, she worked for the government. The government had money and surely wasn't going out of business!

But Mary was mistaken on one point. She forgot that every government's money comes from its people, so while the government didn't go out of business, it certainly didn't have as much money to spend.

When Mary got her notice, she was incredulous and indignant. There must be some mistake, she insisted. She could not believe after working so many years at this job, that she could be treated like this! She felt cruelly treated and betrayed. She stormed home and stewed in her anger, disappointment, and fear.

For some time, Susan had been paying close attention to the downturn in the economy and, in response, had slowly converted her business to principally handling discounted merchandise. During her years of experience, she had noticed in hard times that people spend money on necessities, not luxuries. She believed this economic slump represented an enormous opportunity and prepared to take advantage of it.

When the worst of it hit, she found herself managing a booming business and was hard-pressed to keep up with the flood of orders for her products. With widespread unemployment, the job market was extremely competitive, so she took care to hire only the very best personnel to help her company grow.

Being motivated more by mercy than concern for her company, she also offered Mary a well-paying job high in the organization, but Mary flatly refused. Mary desperately hoped to get another "safe" government job and believed that day couldn't be far away. She still believed Susan's "half-cocked" enterprise was doomed for failure and that Susan would one day learn her lesson.

Not many years afterward, Susan sold her business and was able to retire on the proceeds. She moved away and spent the rest of her life as she had the first—trying new things and living life to the fullest.

Mary eventually got another government job, which, in all fairness, paid a bit better but she didn't like as much. She worked at that job until she was an old woman and outwardly maintained a firm adherence to her "better safe than sorry" philosophy.

Inwardly, though, she constantly worried. If she lost her job once, could it happen again? For the first time, she began to wonder if Susan hadn't been right all along. For years Susan had exposed herself to a multitude of situations while Mary had played it safe.

Like a child that has never been exposed to sickness, Mary built no immunity to hardship and defeat. When it finally came, it nearly destroyed her. Had she been wrong to play it safe all those years? She wondered. What would her life have been like if she had taken more risks?

She sighed, knowing she would never learn the answer.

Have you suffered defeat? Have you failed? Has your social or economic world come crashing down around you?

Good! Congratulations! You now belong to the very exclusive group of people who have tried—those who have made the attempt to do something with their lives. It's much easier to do nothing, to not reach out and take a risk, but you chose to stand up and be counted among the bold.

But you failed.

The Nature of Failure

All failure is constructed mainly of mistakes, sometimes with a bit of misfortune thrown into the mixture. Life didn't turn out as you expected. Now you long for the security and warmth that a life of inaction would bring. But you must not take that path. You must continue to try, because there is no security in avoiding risk.

It has been said that the greatest risk a person can take is taking no risks, and a truer statement does not exist.

The man who refuses to invest or save his money is risking having nothing to sustain him in his retirement. The woman who won't start a business is gambling that her present employer will always be in business or that she will never be fired. The man who is afraid of rejection and never takes a chance on love is betting that he will not wind up a lonely old man.

It is impossible to live without risk. The difference is that some recognize this fact and some hope it's not true. Fairy-tale thinkers hope it's not true because failure hurts tremendously. It's easier to think that there must be a way to avoid it. When one fails, it seems as if all is lost. Failure often means the death of a dream and the realization of a nightmare.

The Advantage of Failure

To say failure can be a nightmare is not the same thing as saying no good can come from it. Can you gain anything by failing? What power could there possibly be in failing a test, being rejected in a date proposal, or not winning an election? The answer is through such trials, you can gain the one thing that cannot be gotten without making the attempt—experience.

What value is experience? Immense value! Why? Because the next time you make your attempt, you will proceed with the confidence that only experience brings. The situation will already look familiar to you. You will have the advantage of knowing the battlefield.

> *Failure often means the death of a dream and the realization of a nightmare.*

Every good warrior studies the ground of the coming battle because it can mean the difference between life and death. When you once again encounter a situation such as the one in which you last failed, you will not be caught by surprise. You will not be intimidated by unfamiliar territory. You might be caught by surprise in another situation, but this one will never daunt you again.

"But I was fired from my last job!"

You are in good company! Many of the world's most successful people have been fired from at least one job because they didn't fit in or conform to status quo. Their mind was usually somewhere else. (If you're at work and your mind is consistently elsewhere, your body probably should be also.)

Many successful businesses were started by people who were fired from their last job. Losing their job was the impetus they needed to begin working on their dream.

"But my business failed!"

Then you will be much more qualified to start or manage a business than someone who has never run a business, since you now know what not to do!

"My marriage failed."

Why not evaluate what went wrong in the last relationship through counseling, education, and prayer? Why not analyze your mistakes (yes, you made some too), learn from them, and resolve to either repair the old relationship or not to repeat the same mistakes in a new relationship?

In failure, you can employ the Power of Choice. You can choose whether you will let this failure defeat or inspire you.

The Perspective of Failure

Rather than being defeated by your situation, picture it as a mere chapter in the amazing story of your life. Can you see it? First our hero goes through many tribulations and trials. Almost all hope is lost. It looks like our hero is beaten. But does he accept this defeat? No! A thousand times no! Instead, he sets his jaw and marches resolutely toward his goal, halting at nothing. No amount of pain, setback, or discouragement stops our hero from reaching the goal before him. At the end of his (your?) story, he basks in the victory of a long and difficult journey.

With this in mind, you must ask yourself a couple of questions.

The first is: Am I avoiding failure? Of course, no one seeks failure. Success is infinitely more attractive and enjoyable, but, if you are to succeed, you must not, at any cost, shy away from risk simply because of possible failure. If you do, ironically, you are ensuring your failure. Instead, you must continue to risk, to make the attempt, to dare to scale the mountain to the next challenge of your journey.

The second question is: Am I failing enough in life? There are many successful salesmen who know that statistically, they must experience a certain number of rejections before they will make their sale. Because they know this, they count their rejections, getting more and more excited as the rejections pile up. They know the odds are that the sale is right around the corner.

They are not foolish enough to believe in luck. No, they base their optimism on the numbers alone. They calculate the number of rejections they must receive to get one sale and then estimate the total number of sales calls they will need to achieve their goals.

In the same way, it is an undeniable fact of life that if you are not experiencing failure, then you are simply not attempting enough. Write it down. Memorize it. Drill it into your mind. You must experience failure in order to have success. There is no other way.

Again, no one is saying that you should court failure or enjoy it. What you must do is accept it as an unpleasant, but necessary, part of your success journey.

Conclusion

Failure is a harsh tutor, much the same as a stern piano instructor of old who raps his students on the knuckles when they err. Failure also raps his students' knuckles, warning

Rather than being defeated by your situation, picture it as a mere chapter in the amazing story of your life.

them not to repeat their mistakes lest they once again experience the same painful result.

The primary objective of Failure, though, is to rid your life of his presence. The teacher, Failure, seeks to make himself obsolete so that his student will be the master instrumentalist and no longer need his instruction.

The question remains, though. Will you quit your music lessons because the master is too cruel, or will you continue, knowing there is no better instructor? Will you employ the Power of Failure?

THE POWER OF BELIEF

An accomplished singer effortlessly glided through his encore performance. The virtuoso's range seemed to have no boundaries. His voice repeatedly leaped into the stratosphere and then plunged into the depths within just a single measure. As he ended the piece with a spirited crescendo, the crowd rose to its feet, filling the auditorium with thunderous applause.

Afterward, he sat at a small table just outside the concert hall, kindly signing autograph after autograph. As the line grew shorter, a young man nervously approached the singer. The singer looked up at the man in anticipation of an autograph request, but the man shook his head.

"It is not an autograph that I seek from you tonight, sir," said the young man. "It is something of far greater value."

Somewhat taken aback, the singer fixed his gaze on the young man. Something about him looked vaguely familiar. A face from long ago, perhaps?

"Don't you recognize me?" said the young man. "We attended school together many years ago. You were older than I, but we were both trained by the same master and considered to possess similar abilities."

"Yes! Yes!" cried the virtuoso. "How good it is to see you again after so many years! I would love to be of service to you in any way that I can. What is it that I may do for you?"

The young man's eyes glinted as he replied, "It is neither boon nor favor I would seek of you tonight, for it is the gift of your counsel alone that I seek."

"I would gladly give you any counsel that I may," answered the singer graciously.

"I would ask that you tell me," continued the young man hesitantly, "the secret of your success."

"Why, we attended the same school! Surely you know every secret as well as I! Why would you ask such a thing, my friend?"

As they spoke, a small crowd gathered to listen. The young man looked about the crowd self-consciously. Then, hardening his resolve, he pounded his fist on the table and cried, "Yes, we did attend the same school! We were taught by the same master. We competed in the same competitions and I even beat you several times. I know that you are neither more talented, educated, nor skilled than I am, and yet you are successful and I am still struggling!"

The small crowd eyed the young man with suspicion and annoyance. Who was this man to bother the virtuoso? What right did he have to raise his voice to the master?

The young man made as though to move away from the crowd, but the virtuoso reached out and gently took hold of his arm.

"No, please stay, my friend," said the singer. "Your words are refreshing. It takes courage to speak with such honesty.

"Since you have been so forthright with me, I will return the favor. I agree with you that you have just as much talent as I do and remember also that you did indeed beat me in several competitions.

"But it is not talent, education, or skill that you need. What you lack is belief. What you lack is an unwavering confidence in the very depths of your being that you belong at the top of your profession."

"That's easy for you to say!" said one of the onlookers. "You're one of the best singers in the world."

The crowd murmured in agreement, feeling that an excellent point had been made.

The virtuoso smiled and said, "I don't believe in myself because I am known as one of the best singers in the world. I am known as one of the best singers in the world because I believe in myself."

The young man sneered and said, "You certainly seem to think a lot of yourself."

"Young man," replied the singer, "if I didn't believe in myself, why should anyone else?"

If you believe in yourself, that is certainly no guarantee that you will achieve success. You may still need to develop your skills, you may need more education, or you may need more experience. But it is guaranteed that you will not be successful if you do not believe in yourself. If you don't believe you can, you're right.

One of the first and most important factors in the principle of belief is that people always tend to believe that which is easiest to believe.

It's emotionally easier to believe that the perfect mate exists out there somewhere than to work on the marriage you are in now. It is easier to believe that the reason your business is failing is because the economy is bad or because you got a bad break. It is easier to believe life has been unfair than to take responsibility and admit fault.

People who are successful employ the Power of Mind and the Power of Choice to discern the truth about their situation without regard to emotion. They rationally evaluate their circumstances and determine the best course of action while maintaining their belief in themselves and the world around them.

What a person believes about himself, about other people, and the world in which he lives will determine how he acts and interacts on a daily basis. If he does not believe he can succeed, he will not be motivated and his work will not be passionate. He will not be open to exploring possibilities, options, and ideas that may lead to accomplishment. If one does not cultivate an attitude of belief, success can only be accidental, rather than achieved; and accidental success is always incidental and short-lived.

No successful person is ever surprised by his success. He may be somewhat taken aback that his plan worked as well as it did, but he is not surprised by the success itself. He always believed it would work, or why else would he have suffered the hard work and long hours it took to bring his idea into reality?

Believe in Yourself

Take a moment and think about what you really believe about yourself. The question is not what do you tell yourself, but, in your heart of hearts, when no one else is around, what do you believe?

Understand that everyone has secret fears and doubts about themselves. Even the most successful business people, actors, and singers have doubts at times. But all successful people possess an abiding faith that lies underneath all the surface doubts. Such belief is essential for success.

But there is a tremendous difference in believing in one's self and believing in one's abilities. You must not believe primarily in your ability. You must not trust only in your talent. You must not have faith solely in your education; nor in how smart, good-looking, witty, or charming you are. All such things can and will fail you. What you must believe is that, beyond all external measure, you have what it takes to ultimately succeed.

This is not to say that you won't need ability or talent. (It is typical of fairy-tale thinkers to believe that there is no need for training, education, talent, or skill. They believe one only needs enough luck.) But, while aptitude is extremely important, the foundation of all success rests in belief.

This is so because there will be times when it seems no one else believes in you. In those times, you will still need to believe in yourself, no matter what external circumstances are telling you. No matter what criticism you receive, no matter what failure you have experienced, no matter what rejection you face, you must still believe in yourself.

What you believe about yourself will also determine what others believe about you and how they treat you. It doesn't matter how you look or what you wear. It doesn't matter what school you attended or if you never attended any school.

It doesn't matter what color your skin is, where you live, or what you do for a living. You are the one who determines whether or not you are respected by the way you carry yourself. People will follow your lead in regard to how you are to be treated. If you do not believe that you are worthy of respect, others will follow suit and treat you accordingly. If you demand respect, not by arrogance or insolence, but by a confident attitude in forwarding your agenda, others will adjust their opinion about you correspondingly.

Be sure not to confuse belief with conceit and arrogance. They are really just forms of insecurity which attempt to disguise themselves in bravado. Arrogant people are rude and seek to bolster their own sagging confidence by demeaning others.

Conversely, self-belief is a humble, deep-seated conviction of worth that allows recognition of one's own shortcomings. It is a confidence that retains an openness to constructive criticism. True self-belief and confidence allow for appreciation of another's accomplishment and worth without feeling threatened.

Just as in most other areas of your life, belief also is a choice. Do you lack that belief? Don't worry! It is available to everyone. While it is true that some people have had others in their lives who have nurtured and encouraged them, that doesn't mean, if you didn't have that advantage, that you must now do without. It just means that you must be your own encourager.

Use the Power of Mind to create the mental picture of who you would like to be. See yourself in a great marriage, running a successful company, or living whatever type of life you dream of. Then rid yourself of all talk, both inside your head and out, that contradicts this picture. Read articles and books that will support the belief that you can be this person, and don't let go of that image. Of course, you will have to do much more to make this picture a reality than just dream and believe, but to foster your self-belief, you must first envision a successful "you."

As you develop your mental picture, you can expect to be assaulted with multiple failures. When this happens, you will be tempted to re-adopt your old picture of yourself. The negative voices will attempt to rise again.

"See? Who are you kidding? You will never be successful. Only certain people have successful relationships. You never have won and you never will. You are a loser. Your company will fail. You will never achieve your sales quota. You will never find love and will wind up old, lonely, and broke."

Sound familiar? When the doubt comes, be prepared for the assault by being ready to employ the Power of Choice. Harden your will and believe that you are becoming the fulfillment of your aspirations. Refer to your plan and look at the small steps that you have been able to achieve in pursuit of your dream. You must aggressively battle self-doubt or it will defeat you.

In the end, the most important person that should believe in you is you. Don't ever let anyone talk you out of that belief, for it is a powerful tool in creating the success you desire.

Believe in Other People

It is important to cultivate an attitude of belief in other people, because not doing so will shadow your thinking and cause you to miss opportunities. If you believe that most people are trying to wrong you, then you will be less likely to take risks. If you believe that most people are disinclined to help you, then you will be less likely to ask for assistance.

Do you believe that people are generally nice, or that people are unkind? Are people generous, or are they stingy? You will find that what you believe about other people will most often prove true. How can this be true when everyone believes differently? Because it is human nature to search for, and produce, evidence to support our core beliefs.

One person experiences rudeness from a store clerk and thinks, "Clerks are always rude!" Another person is rendered aid when broken down on the side of the road and thinks, "See! That's just how people are." Someone else is taken advantage of in a business deal and thinks, "People certainly will swindle you if given half a chance!"

Each person will continue to experience incidents that will support his core beliefs and will even act in such a way so as to produce his presuppositions. If you feel the store clerk is going to be rude to you, you are likely to be less than friendly before a word has been exchanged.

People will find a way to validate their beliefs because it is important to feel they made the right decisions. Because it is emotionally difficult and strenuous to reevaluate a core belief, most people do their best to avoid it.

But what if, instead of thinking the worst of people, you developed the habit of thinking the best? It is always better to be disappointed, believing the best of people, than be proven right while believing the worst.

True, you will occasionally be disappointed, but you will find that your positive expectation of people will consistently produce better performance and attitudes from those you encounter.

It is vital that you develop a strong belief in people because they are a large part of your success. No man succeeds alone; it is always with the partnership of many people. In order to experience success, you must become a people-builder. You must learn to believe in the people with whom you interact daily—your spouse, coworkers, employees, committee members—all are vital in the implementation and completion of your plan for success.

People need to know that you believe in them, and the only way for them to do so is for you

> *It is vital that you develop a strong belief in people because they are a large part of your success.*

to tell them, not once but many times, in as many different ways as you can conceive. Have you ever thought that it should be enough for you just to think well of those around you without having to tell them? You cannot claim to believe in the people around you if you are not verbally communicating that belief.

The nature of belief is the same as that of love. If a man claims he loves his children, but never expresses that love, then his love is incomplete, at best. In the same way, belief must be offered daily in the form of verbal encouragement, communicating that you know your associate, friend, spouse, business partner, or whoever will ultimately succeed.

But what if you feel you can't believe in them? What if they aren't talented? What if they aren't that bright? What if they are inept? Is lying to them the answer?

No, honesty regarding people's faults is important, but in most cases, it is encouragement, not criticism, that is lacking. By far, most people perform better if they are surrounded by people who believe in them rather than by people who are constantly pointing out their faults. Rather than focusing on what is wrong, focus on what is right.

Remember that there is a tremendous difference in believing in a person and believing in a person's abilities. It is important to communicate to those around you that, beyond any present difficulties they may be experiencing, you see the value of who they are now and the potential of what they can become.

Still, you will not change the world by believing in people. There are people who are locked into destructive patterns who have grown comfortable in mediocrity and refuse to change. Each one must choose for himself what he believes about himself.

You should also remember to continue to practice the use of wisdom in relationships and business dealings. Not everyone is as trustworthy and honest as you might like. But, while it is true that there are certainly people in the world who would seek to harm you, it is also true that most people are relatively honest and are not out to take advantage of you. It is an ego-crushing fact of life that people are usually worried about themselves and don't think much about you at all.

Practicing an attitude of belief in other people will certainly not change the whole world, but it will certainly improve yours.

*It is important to communicate
to those around you that,
beyond any present difficulties
they may be experiencing,
you see the value of who they
are now and the potential
of what they can become.*

Believe in Your World

Things just aren't how they used to be. There are not any eligible marriage partners out there. The economy is reeling. Everyone is getting divorced these days. Nobody is buying, selling, or hiring. Prices are too high. Prices are too low. Most people are depressed. The market is too weak; it's a buyer's market. The market is too strong; it's a seller's market.

If you are even slightly prone to such beliefs, you must strenuously and vigorously expel all such thinking from your life. Not believing the best about the world in which you live will affect your life in the same way that not believing the best of people will—your negative attitude will shadow your thinking and cause you to miss opportunities.

If you believe the economy is soft, you will not try as hard. After all, why make a sales call if people don't have the money to buy?

If you believe that most marriages don't last, then why should you try to improve your own? If your marriage is doomed anyway, then why bother with marriage counseling?

So, do you just turn off your mind and go about in some positive-thinking, self-deluded daze? No. Again, believing in the world around you is not turning off your mind, but evaluating and objectifying the given situations, and then deciding what you are going to believe.

Most people never look past their first impression. They hear the economy is bad or the market is slow and they just blindly accept the notion that these things are bad news. They never realize there might be another perspective that is just as valid as the original one with which they were presented.

Yes, the economy may have slowed, but is that necessarily bad news for the person who is actively utilizing the Seven Powers? By no means! It will definitely mean changes, but some of those changes might include buying at a discount from people looking to liquidate quickly. It might mean using one's creativity to seek business ideas that thrive in times of economic downturn. Not everybody becomes poor during a poor economy. Some people, believing that such times hold vast opportunity, grow quite wealthy.

Conclusion

No amount of belief alone will change the world. Without the implementation of the other six powers, the Power of Belief is just wishful or fairy-tale thinking.

> *Somewhere deep within you, however faint, lies the belief that you are able and destined to achieve.*

You will not believe yourself into prosperity, love, and longevity. There is no magic and no amount of belief by itself will change your life for the better.

But without the Power of Belief, the other six powers are worthless. The Power of Belief is the fuel that drives the other powers. It is the spark that ignites the flame of your creativity, imagination, and drive.

Somewhere deep within you, however faint, lies the belief that you are able and destined to achieve. You must grasp that belief, nurture it, and turn it into a powerful tool for your success. You must capture and harness that belief and make it serve your objectives.

The Power of Belief is your secret weapon. It is your hidden force that is the difference between success and failure. Everyone who has ever succeeded, in whatever field you can name, has employed the Power of Belief.

Now it is your turn to unleash that same power and be named among the other greats of the world who have dared to believe.

THE POWER OF CHARACTER

In the past twenty-five years of running the king's armory, Henry Matthews had never encountered a problem such as this. Most of the men in his charge had been with him for many years and he knew and trusted them like his own family. Others had only recently joined his staff. It was difficult to know who the traitor was.

He had narrowed his suspects to two of the newer men, but how could he know which one was the guilty party? How could he be sure that it wasn't both? He had to know. In the business of designing and manufacturing the king's weaponry, loyalty was not an option; it was a mandate.

Because of the recent unpleasantness with a neighboring country, this was a most crucial time in the kingdom. The king had commanded Henry to ready the armory in preparation for war and had approved several new weapon designs for manufacture. These new weapons might mean the difference between winning and losing the war.

Henry had suspected for some time that his designs might be falling into the hands of the king's enemies, but now the severity of the problem was multiplied in light of the upcoming war.

If the king were to discover this breach in security, it might not only mean Henry's position; it might mean his life. Something had to be done.

He arranged a meeting to discuss the matter with his old friend, Sir Reginald, who served as the chief of guards. Sir Reginald's loyalty was unquestioned and he was one of the very few people Henry knew he could trust beyond a doubt.

Henry arrived at the guard house exactly on time and greeted his friend. Sir Reginald shook his hand warmly and walked Henry over to a couple of wooden chairs near the hearth. They chatted for a while about work and the happenings in each other's family.

After they dispensed with the small talk, Henry briefly laid out his problem for his friend. Sir Reginald listened attentively, nodding his head and occasionally asking a clarifying question.

"Well, what do you think I should do, Sir Reginald?"

"I'm not sure, Henry," answered the soldier. "This is not the sort of problem we deal with around here, so I'm certainly no expert. I know you wouldn't want to publicize this. It could be dangerous for you and make it more difficult to catch the spy. Have you thought about inquiring of the king's wise men?"

"Sure, I've thought about it, but they would want an investigation and I'd rather not have someone from the outside hanging around asking everyone a lot of questions. It would look pretty bad to the king's court and it could destroy morale at a time when we all need to be operating at our top performance."

"I see what you mean. I don't suppose you could just fire your craftsmen and hire a new staff?"

"No, no. The craft of weaponry takes years to master and with the coming war, we wouldn't have the time. Besides, I'm pretty sure the spy would have to be somebody in the armory's bookkeeping department that would have access to my drawings and plans."

"You have a bookkeeping department?" Sir Reginald asked in surprise. "I thought all you did was make swords and shields."

"I wish it were that simple," said Henry, smiling. He looked thoughtful for a moment and then continued. "Another reason I wouldn't let anyone go is that it would be unfair to punish the innocent along with the guilty. I certainly don't want to demonstrate the same disloyalty that I suspect of at least one of them. If my people think I'm the sort of person that would indiscriminately fire an innocent person, then they will think they might be next. It's not the sort of policy that will build teamwork loyalty.

"As you know, one of the king's foundational principles is, 'Character is consistent. If it applies in one area of your life, it applies in all areas, to one degree or another.' I believe in character and want to abide by that principle, just like everyone else."

"Oh yes!" said Sir Reginald laughing. "I've only heard you say that about a thousand times. It's one of the things that I like about you.

"But regarding your problem, I'm not sure that you have many more options, Henry. What else can you do?"

"Hmmm?" answered Henry, pulling himself back from another thought. "Oh, yes, certainly not many more options."

Rising, he stuck out his hand. "I've got to run now and work on an idea. Thanks so much for this meeting. It has been most helpful... most helpful indeed."

As Henry walked briskly from the room, Sir Reginald shook his head and chuckled. "If I know Henry, he's onto something and will have this problem handled soon enough!"

When Henry arrived at the armory that afternoon, he went directly to his accounting office and spoke to the first of his suspects

"Ben," he said. "I need you to resubmit last quarter's inventory for me."

"What's wrong, boss? Something didn't add up?"

"No, no. Not that at all," said Henry, smiling. "No, I need you to make some of this inventory disappear. With the coming war, we'll need a lot more supplies and I want to be sure that we get them. These numbers make it appear that we have more inventory than I'd like the Department of Requisitions to think we have."

"Hmmm, I see what you mean," Ben said uncertainly. "What do you want me to do with the report?"

"Well, I don't know. Can you think of any expenses or perhaps some inventory allotments that maybe you forgot to mention in your last report?" Henry asked, still smiling.

"You know that might not be, well, exactly on the level, don't you, sir?" the young accountant asked, grinning slightly.

"Well, you just let me worry about that, Ben. As you know, loyalty is important in this kingdom and I need to know if you're with me on this. Sure, I'm asking you to do a little 'creative accounting' for me, but we're a tight family here and loyalty is always rewarded. And disloyalty..." he paused and the smile faded for just a moment, "disloyalty is dealt with accordingly."

The implication was obvious.

"Can I count on you, Ben?" Henry asked, sticking out his hand.

Ben smiled and shook Henry's hand. "Sure thing, boss. I won't let you down!"

Henry found his other suspect coming out of his office.

"Oh, good, Tom! I'm glad I ran into you," Henry said. "Just wanted to check with you on a little matter."

Once again Henry made his request that the quarterly report be altered to reflect more expenses and less inventory. He made it clear to Tom that not to comply would bring into question his loyalty at a time when loyalty was of paramount importance. He colored his comments with the subtle hint that not to submit might lead to the termination of Tom's employment.

As he spoke, the young man's expression became troubled.

"Sir, I haven't known you all that long, so maybe I'm not understanding you. You're saying that either I alter my report to reflect untruth or I might lose my job?"

"Tom, that's a pretty harsh way to put it, but I have to know that you are a team player. Either you are with us and are willing to do your part, or maybe you don't need to be on my team."

Tom stiffened immediately and said, "Sir, I'll clean out my desk and be gone within the hour."

"Do you mean you're willing to lose your job over this?" Henry asked incredulously.

"It looks like I'm going to have to, sir," said the young man solemnly, "because I'm not altering that report."

Henry smiled broadly. He had just discovered his man.

Once again Henry sat in front of the hearth of his good friend. "That's some story, Henry," said Sir Reginald, smiling appreciatively. "You have quite a head on your shoulders."

"Oh, I don't know about that," Henry said. "It was that conversation we had the other day that gave me the idea. Remember? 'Character is consistent. If it applies in one area of your life, it applies in all areas, to one degree or another.'

"I figured if a man would be willing to cheat and lie for my company so he could keep his job, then he would probably be willing to cheat and lie for someone else's company so he could line his pockets.

"After I spoke with both men, I had enough information to search Ben's office. We found a lot of documents that he had no business having. He was escorted out immediately. We found out later that Ben had strong ties to our enemy."

"That's great," said Sir Reginald. "But whatever happened to Tom?"

"Tom? Tom got promoted!" Henry answered, laughing. "The way I figure it, if a man is willing to lose his job in order to protect his integrity, that's the kind of man I want on my team!"

Just as with any of the other Seven Powers, character can be built and developed. It is the most overlooked and undervalued of the Seven Powers. It is the most difficult to develop—and the most essential. It is the foundation upon which all the other six powers are built.

All character is a choice. One can choose the quality of one's character just as one can choose which shirt to wear. No one is born with good character. It does not function the same as personality or temperament. One cannot change one's tendency to be outgoing but can absolutely change one's character.

But why bother? Is it really that important? Is it a given that such people always do better in life, or do you believe that "nice guys finish last"? Many people that have lacked character have certainly attained success, haven't they?

Many most definitely have, if you measure success from a fairy-tale perspective, but fortunately, life isn't a fairy tale. It is built from many absolute truths, such as the law of sowing and reaping, or "what goes around, comes around."

If a person has cheated and stolen his way to the top of his profession, he is almost ensuring that he will not stay there because he lacks the foundation to sustain his success. It is as if he built a tall building on a foundation of sand so that when any instability occurs, the whole building crumbles.

He cannot count on friendship or loyalty to save him, because no one trusts him and he trusts no one. He cannot count on money to save him because, if he took it from someone, someone else can take it from him.

If a person of bad character spends a lifetime in questionable dealing, poor work habits, unfaithfulness, and cowardice, who in the world would want to deal with him again? He is a prisoner of his own design.

Have you ever noticed how a person's character and reputation are intrinsically connected? It is impossible to have bad character and not be known for those qualities. In the same way, you cannot help being known for good character, if you possess it.

But character is not just something one does to achieve and maintain success.

Being a person of character is something you do for yourself, and not for anyone else. You are the one that will have to live with the type of person you are. When you work on your character, you are building your life from the ground up.

Persistence

How can anyone succeed without developing persistence? It is the voice that commands you forward when everything inside screams at you to quit. It is the tenacity you need to see a project to the end. It is the immovable resolve that causes you to follow through.

Everyone has desire; few have persistence.

Everyone has desire; few have persistence. In any given endeavor, much of your competition will be eliminated simply because they did not persist.

How many people begin an exercise regimen only to abandon it after a few months? How many people begin to change their diet, learn a foreign language, or save some money, only to give up when it becomes difficult? How many people read a book, apply its principles for a few weeks, and slip back into the same, old, mental ruts?

So, how does one develop persistence?

First, choose which efforts or actions are worth continuing. Is there a reward if you persist? There is no value or virtue in persisting in an action that will only bring harm. Who would do such a thing, you ask?

How many people are, at this very moment, in destructive and dangerous relationships simply because they feel if they just wait a little longer, it will get better? How many people are in dead-end jobs because they believe it's not right to quit a job?

After you determine that persisting in an action is worth your effort, decide to continue. It's that simple. When you eliminate the option of quitting, it makes persisting much easier.

Easier, but never easy. Sometimes persistence is a daily decision; sometimes it's hourly. But it's important to remember that persistence is a habit that can be learned. As you develop the trait of persistence, you will unlearn the tendency to quit and find it natural to continue.

Deep within you, buried far down in your soul, is an iron will, a piece of steel that you can access anytime you reach deep enough. It will lend you the strength to persist until you are victorious. Harden your will. Strengthen your resolve. Put one foot in front of the other until you have conquered.

Courage

Yes, it can be defined as the hero jumping into the fray against overwhelming odds, but more often it's the widowed mother working two jobs to care for her children. It's the foster-parents caring for children from troubled homes. It's the student putting herself through school by working part-time jobs. It's the couple attending counseling for years to mend a troubled marriage. It's a policeman patrolling his beat day after day. It's the entrepreneur working eighty- or ninety-hour weeks for years in order to provide for his family.

Courage is never the absence of fear, but doing one's duty in the face of fear; marching on resolutely, persisting in one's responsibility, without regard to one's own well-being.

In a world of people who run at the first sign of discomfort or inconvenience, courageous people are desperately needed. Most of them will never have a book written about them. Most of them will never have songs sung in their honor. Most of their names will never be known. But they are heroes nonetheless, because they had a choice, and they chose courage.

They chose to sacrifice their desires, their safety, their financial well-being, their health, and more—all because they wanted to do what they felt was right.

Where would this world be without such people? What would society be like? It would consist of a group of self-centered babies who are only concerned with what pleases them at the moment.

No marriages would last. Children would be left untended and cast away. The weak would be overrun and defenseless. Homes would be left to burn. There would be no order, only chaos.

Such a description might sound very much like society today, and yet, there are the courageous: those faceless heroes who daily go about their business, sacrificing themselves so that another might have food, shelter, protection, and security.

Does one need courage to succeed? Without a doubt. The success journey is not for the faint of heart. It is not for the weak-willed. It is for the brave who would dare change their destiny and the destiny of others by stepping up and giving their best when they don't feel like it, when the whole world is against them, when they are afraid, tired, weak, and hungry.

Are you one of the brave? Will you act courageously when called upon? How will you act when the unexpected commands your time and resources?

Do not think for one minute that you do not have what it takes. Within every man, woman, and child lies the seed of greatness that waits only for the moment it is demanded. You have within you that greatness; the spark of courage.

Integrity

Where is the man who will do the right thing, no matter what the cost? Is there anyone who will act in integrity even if it means losing a job or an important business deal? Where is the woman who would be willing to act in openness and honesty if she knew it meant losing a significant relationship or a large sum of money? Are there still people in this world who would sacrifice their pride, relationships, or profit in order to maintain their integrity? Are you such a person?

Integrity is a foreign concept to the fairy-tale thinker. He will always compromise his ethics today, believing he will make everything right when his ship finally comes in. Doing so, he amasses a tremendous integrity debt that he will someday have to pay. One day his reputation will catch up with him and prevent the success he hopes to encounter.

Fairy-tale thinkers hope their omission of doing the right thing will be overlooked or forgotten by those they wrong. They try to quickly put their fault out of their minds and like to think everyone else has done the same.

But what *is* integrity?

Integrity is doing the right thing when you don't have to—when no one else is looking or will ever know—when there will be no congratulations or recognition for having done so.

Suppose you are a salesman who discovers you have accidentally overcharged your customer months after the sale. The customer did not seem to notice and appears to be perfectly satisfied with the product, service, and transaction.

In such a situation, you have several choices. Do you keep your mouth shut and continue to charge the customer that price from that point on? How about not mentioning the error to the customer this time but correcting the price in future sales?

Or how about electing to take ownership of the mistake and confessing your error to the customer? This option would almost certainly mean lowering your sales volume and incurring a loss in commission.

Fairy-tale thinkers cannot see the reason in the latter thinking at all. They think that every dime in their pocket should stay there because it must have been meant to be. The fairy-tale thinker believes that if the customer was stupid enough to pay the amount, then why not take it? He sees this as a mini-ship coming in and considers it a lucky break.

He reasons that confessing his error might make the situation even worse. What if the customer got upset and felt he was taken advantage of? What if he embarrassed the customer by pointing out an error that the customer did not catch himself?

What the fairy-tale thinker is missing, though, is the big picture. Most likely, the customer will be impressed with the salesman's honesty and forthrightness in admitting the error. This probably will strengthen the customer's relationship with the salesman because now he knows that the salesman can be trusted. Any monetary loss incurred will undoubtedly be recouped in future sales.

Integrity is doing the right thing no matter what it costs you. Very often, you will find that the cost is your pride. How many marriages could be saved if the couple cultivated the practice of apology and forgiveness? How many business partnerships would survive and flourish if the owners would own their mistakes? How many churches would prosper if members would admit fault?

Have you ever apologized to someone whom you have offended, maybe a stranger or business acquaintance you don't know that well? Yes, you probably were offended as well, but take a moment to try thinking of the situation from the other person's perspective. How did you wrong them? Now, this is the part that hurts: If you wronged them at all, no matter for what reason, then you owe them a sincere apology. No wrong perpetrated on another person is justified by the wrong they did to you. You are responsible for your actions independent of other people's actions.

Learn to recognize the childish voices in your head telling you that the other person started it or you had a right to hit them (literally or figuratively) because they struck you first. Learn to recognize the voices for what they are: immature attempts to justify a wrong you committed.

Practicing the forgotten art of repentance places you in the position of power because you are the one who controls the direction of the conversation. By doing so, you might be able to get the conversation back on track toward a productive end, such as a sale or a reconciled relationship.

Asking for forgiveness is not displaying weakness, but strength. You are the one taking the more mature approach to ending the conflict. Even if the relationship goes no further, you have the knowledge that you did the right thing.

Everyone interested in pursuing a successful life should pay close attention to developing integrity. To guard your integrity is to guard the trust others place in you. To guard that trust is to guard your success, because all relationships— professional, romantic, family, or social—are built on trust.

What if you truly desire to do the right thing, but are not sure what the right thing is? When in doubt as to which action you should take, there are several ways you might discern the correct path:

- Make all decisions based on how you will feel about that action in ten years. Will you be proud or ashamed?
- Apply the Golden Rule, acting as you would like another to treat you. If you were in the other person's shoes, what would you like to have done to/for you?
- Get the opinion of people whose integrity you admire. You might not like the answer they give, but you should receive valuable insight.

The most important question with regard to integrity, though, is why should one have integrity?

The most important answer to that question is that it defines who you are. Yes, it most definitely defines what other people think of you. It absolutely determines the degree of success you obtain. But much more significantly, it delineates the person that you are.

At the end of the day or the end of your life, it is important to be comfortable with the life you lived. Certainly no one is perfect, but there are those who live with a passion for integrity.

Many things may happen to you in this life and in your job. Catastrophe may strike. Disaster may fall. You can and will make many mistakes, but nobody, nobody, can take away how you respond to those events. Did you act with honor? Did you respond in integrity? How you respond to those events is what defines whether or not you are a person of integrity.

Discipline

In this world there are the masters and the mastered.

The masters are individuals who have incrementally taken control over an area in their lives and subjected that area to their will.

For example, one who would aspire to become a classical pianist must spend untold hours meticulously forcing one's fingers not only to press the correct key, but also to execute the note at the right time with exactly the right amount of pressure. Every single note in every musical piece has a specific way that it should be played, in addition to any expression the individual pianist might add. One might be born with the aural sensitivity and manual dexterity needed to train to become a classical pianist, but it is discipline that furnishes the skill needed to master the instrument.

For that reason alone, every child should have the opportunity to learn to paint, play an instrument, or play an organized sport. To engage in such activities over a long period of time is to learn the secret of discipline. To spend time in developing such discipline is to make a lifetime investment in character that will translate into other areas of one's life. The student accustomed to spending long hours practicing repetitive scales and exercises will find it easier to focus on studying for exams. The student accustomed to the discipline of regular study normally doesn't have difficulty holding a job.

The mastered of this world, on the other hand, are the fairytale thinkers who allow circumstance, fear, desire, and laziness to dominate them, prohibiting them from success. They never force themselves to do anything unpleasant such as studying, practicing a sales pitch, exercising, or taking a class. They are content to complain about how life has treated them unfairly and whine about never getting ahead. They are quick to tell you they tried that once but it didn't work for them. Strangers to the concept of prolonged, sustained effort to reach a long-term goal, they long for quick, one-time solutions to their problems.

The great majority of them never realize they are slaves; slaves to their own desires, slaves to circumstance, slaves to comfort, slaves to fear.

They are usually carrying an enormous load of consumer debt, as opposed to investment debt, because they did not possess the self-control to live within their means. They wanted the better things of life now and were willing to sell themselves into slavery to get them.

Incidentally, consumer debt is vastly different than investment debt because the motives of both are diametrically opposed. The investor is sacrificing immediate gratification by placing his money where he hopes it will grow and multiply. Conversely, long-term consumer debt is incurred by those who lack the self-control to delay gratification and live within their means. Of course, this is not to be confused with debt incurred from financial emergencies such as a sudden job loss or health failure.

The mastered of the world are often dominated by the tyranny of substance abuse, choosing artificial stimulants rather than creating real-world pleasures in their lives. They are the first to cry that their ailment is beyond their control and that they are the victims of disease. They overlook the fact that countless others have overcome the very same afflictions and weaknesses, choosing instead to turn their lives toward a higher purpose rather than retreat through immediate gratification.

The untold secret is that the masters of this world are cursed with the same weaknesses as everyone else but simply do not allow themselves to use those shortcomings as excuses. They accept the reality that these things must be overcome. They choose to see these afflictions as speedbumps, not brick walls. To them, it does not matter if it is a genetic predisposition, learning disability, behavioral disability, or even if they are not good-looking enough.

Nor do they have their heads in the sand. They are brutally honest with themselves in inventorying and assessing their weaknesses, but they focus their efforts on creating plans to take them over these hurdles, rather than adjusting their lives to allow for them. They know if they are to experience success, they must climb these obstacles.

Freedom only begins when you realize that you were not meant to be mastered, but to master. It begins with the hope that it is possible to be free from that which has mastered you, and the desire to be more than a slave. Every human is born with the knowledge buried deep inside that he was destined for freedom.

Some, however, are willing to trade that freedom for what they hope will be an easier path, but freedom is never easy. It must be bought with hard work, sacrifice, and persistence.

As the subject is pondered, though, the question becomes: Are you a master or one of the mastered? Have you trained yourself in the disciplines in which successful people engage?

> *The masters of this world are cursed with the same weaknesses as everyone else but simply do not allow themselves to use those shortcomings as excuses.*

It has been said that sometimes the question is more important than the answer. Here are several questions to ask yourself in order to help you discern the present level of discipline in your life:

- The discipline of work — Will you work when you don't feel like it; when your body aches, your spirit is weak, and your mind is weary? Do you create opportunities to work, or excuses not to?

- The discipline of sacrifice — Are you an individual that must have everything now, or are you one who forgoes immediate gratification in favor of reaching a greater objective? Will you willingly do without today so that there will be a benefit tomorrow?

- The discipline of body — Are you ruled by your appetite, or have you bent your dietary habits to your will? Is your body your master, craving that which is destructive to its longevity, or do you build and strengthen it with that which will produce the health you desire? Do you train your body for the health you would like to possess tomorrow, or do you think you are different from everyone else and will somehow always have good health just because you happen to now?

- The discipline of personal growth — Do you actively seek out and read books that will stretch your personal limits and challenge you to become more than you are? Are you consistently and habitually accepting challenges to complacency and dormancy in your life?

- The discipline of relationships — Have you made a conscious effort to develop healthy, long-lasting friendships and working relationships, or have you formed your associations by accident? Are the majority of your friendships and work associations a result of chance and proximity, or have you sought to form associations that will lead you where you want to go, both personally and professionally?

- The discipline of speech — Do you carefully guard the words that come out of your mouth, or are you someone that feels the world has a right to hear every thought that happens through your mind? Are you careful to only speak words that will build up those around you, rather than feeling it is your right to express your opinion, no matter how hurtful it may be?

There is no more serious quest than the pursuit of discipline. Discipline represents the skeletal structure of your life. It is the strength that supports all other activity. To forsake discipline is to forsake the strength you will need when times are difficult.

Discipline is the frame around which your house is built. Storms will come with a ferocity that will threaten the integrity of the structure that is your life, seeking to destroy all you have sought and hoped for. Remember, the weaker your discipline, the easier your house will crumble.

Giving

Where would this world be without the untold millions of people who selflessly give their time and resources so others might have better lives? What would it be like to live in a world where everyone tended only to his own welfare and cared nothing for others? Would you like to live in such a world?

Of course, everyone must give attention to the maintenance and support of his own household. Not to do so would be irresponsible and negligent. But a truly successful life must consist of more than simply meeting one's needs and those of one's household. Those who live their lives solely for themselves are inevitably unfulfilled and suffer from feelings of unease. They have a vague sense of dissatisfaction with themselves and usually don't realize the source of their discomfort.

The cause of such a person's unhappiness is that they have not allowed the waters to continue to flow through their lives. Every lake or pond will become stagnant when its waters stand for a long period, having no place to flow. A healthy body of water will not only have streams flowing into it, but will also have outlets through which water can continue flowing. Ponds with no outlet will eventually become stagnant, fetid pools that are poisonous to all wildlife, including fish.

Part of living a life of completion is using a portion of what one has received to help others in need. The person in need is not owed this assistance. It is not the right of the needy to expect that others should come to their aid, but it is the responsibility of those with, to help those without.

Those who practice giving their time, knowledge, and money will unanimously testify that they have received far more than they have given. It is a universal principle that what is sown, will one day be reaped. It is a law just as real as gravity.

But it is truly amazing that fairy-tale thinking can even find its way into the act of giving. There are those who misinterpret and pervert this principle to support their fairy-tale thinking. They believe the law of sowing and reaping is just another way of saying "something wonderful is going to happen to me just because I'm good."

The truth is that the two philosophies could not be further apart. The law of sowing and reaping is an investment vehicle, because those who invest themselves in the act of giving may expect a like return. If, on the other hand, one engages in the fantasy of fairy-tale thinking and believes one's charity will result in a completely unrelated windfall, one will be sorely disappointed.

To think you will get rich because you volunteer at a soup kitchen is as ridiculous as believing you will get corn by planting watermelon seeds. The crop will always reflect the seed. If you think you're going to become a millionaire by feeding the hungry, you are greatly mistaken. If, however, you feel you will receive the gratitude of those you have helped and increased opportunity for additional benevolence in the future, you are most likely correct.

So, what of the person who claims he gave away money and received it back in a greater measure? There is undoubtedly a spiritual truth reflected in such a testimony but, just as profound, is the reality that the act of giving changes the giver. You simply cannot give on a regular basis without being changed. Giving changes your mind and your perspective by freeing you from the bondage of fear and greed.

By giving money away, you are demonstrating that money is not your master. This attitude will allow you the advantage of a clearer perspective in any business deal you engage in, assisting you to make better decisions. It is always easier to make financial decisions when you are not pressured by fear or tantalized by greed. Thus, when one experiences a material increase in response to one's financial benevolence, that increase might very well be the result of changed perspective.

*You are writing your legacy
at this very moment in the
ink of your character.*

Every day someone passionately decries the wrongs and injustices of this world. Every day someone says that something needs to be done to help the hurting. Every day there are those who see the need but take no action.

Compassion is not compassion if no action is taken. To give of one's life is to take a small step toward making this a better world, and a tremendous step in becoming a better person.

Conclusion

Have you ever really looked at a tree? How closely have you examined one? You can tell much of a tree's character by cutting it down and looking at its rings. If you know what you are looking for, you can tell which years it withstood disease, which years it survived terrible storms, and which years it flourished.

If you were to look inside yourself, what could you tell about your character? Does it show damage from years of diseased thinking? Have the storms in your life strengthened and developed your character, or have they served to weaken it?

After all the superficiality is stripped away—your personality, the way you look and dress, your body, even how smart you are—character is what is left over. Have you ever seen someone who used to be beautiful in her younger days, but now her good looks have faded? It is very sad if that person never took the time or trouble to develop her character and is still attempting to trade on a beauty that no longer exists. The same could be said of wealth or wit.

Everything else may let you down, but character lasts forever and is an eternal investment. Every year countless dollars are spent on products and techniques to improve one's appearance, but how much thought or effort is given to improving one's character? To spend time developing character is to invest in the person you are now and forever will be.

Your character is predominantly what you will be remembered for after you are gone. You are writing your legacy at this very moment in the ink of your character. Ask yourself, what will people remember about you? Not, what do you hope people will remember about you, but what will people actually remember?

Fairy-tale thinkers live however their childish fancies dictate and never experience success, but there are no limits for the person of strong character. In good times and bad, it is people of stout character that others look to for leadership and courage. Those who aspire to greatness give thought to their character and realize the Power of Character is a strong force in creating success.

THE FIVE DEADLY ENEMIES

No kingdom has ever existed that did not have enemies. There are essentially two types of enemies. There is the adversary with whom you are at open war, and then there is the far more dangerous enemy—the one that lives within your house, that works for your ruin within the walls of your own home.

You have such an enemy living with you at this very moment; not just one, but five distinct enemies that are unified in their goal, which is your utter destruction. They work in unison, strengthening and enhancing one another's efforts. They are tireless and relentless as they strive to defeat you.

All your life they have hounded you. You have found yourself struggling to maintain and build your kingdom and have been mystified as to why you were failing. Whenever you felt you were beginning to succeed, you looked behind you to find that all you had built was lying in ruins.

They use your best resources against you. They know and exploit all of your weaknesses. Who are these enemies that so viciously attack you?

They are the Lords of Mediocrity.

Each of the lords is the distant cousin and counterfeit of a more noble lord that works for your good. These rogue lords have set up their own small kingdoms within your realm and are constantly at your side, speaking in your ear, subtly attempting to undermine your success by poisoning your mind.

At first glance they appear as friends, greatly resembling their good cousins. They are your constant companions, your confidants, and advisors. They seem to be vigorously working for your good and the good of your kingdom, having only your best interest at heart. But you must not be fooled. You must learn to recognize them for what they are. Each of these enemies must be subdued and made to serve you. You must check their growth and subdue them, bending them to your will.

The first step in defeating any enemy is to recognize him. Powerful is the foe who works in secret. Once your enemy is targeted, you can then begin your own offensive. You can begin to build and strengthen your defenses so your enemy bothers you no more.

Unfortunately, you will never be able to completely rid yourself of the Lords of Mediocrity, since they are so closely related to their worthy cousins. But you can beat them into submission, starve them, and post a guard so that any attempt of theirs to once again rise up against you will be immediately crushed.

At long last, it is time you finally meet the Lords of Mediocrity.

12

THE LORD OF DOUBT

The Lord of Doubt is of a somber, but kindly, disposition. He is the brother of Fear and the distant cousin of Belief. Whenever a decision is to be made, he is there with you. With his head wagging mournfully, he listens compassionately while you excitedly tell him of your dream, plan, and vision. When your initial enthusiasm starts to wane, he puts his arm around your shoulder and sympathetically explains why this simply cannot be done.

"Where are your resources?" he asks. "Isn't it true that you have never done this sort of thing before? Is it wise to begin such a thing at this time in your life? You have so much going on already!"

He continues in the manner of a loving uncle, patiently explaining why your plan will never work. No, it would just be better to continue as you have been and perhaps later another, more suitable, plan will arise.

Yes, you think, that makes perfect sense. Why did you ever think such an idea was possible? Who are you to feel that you could accomplish such a thing? It was a foolish and foolhardy plan. Thank goodness for your good friend, the Lord of Doubt. What would you do without him?

Good question. The answer might just be "anything."

Doubt is not the opposite of belief. Rather, it is inverted belief. It is negative faith. When you doubt, you are still believing in something, but in something negative, rather than something positive. You have made a conscious decision to believe the worst-case scenario, rather then the best.

Doubters excitedly point to the half-empty glass as their proof of why it cannot be done. Believers take note of the half-empty glass, but maintain that despite the empty portion (and sometimes because of it), their plan will succeed. This type of belief drives the doubters of the world crazy. Since they are unable to see it, it must not be possible.

There are only two types of people in the world: those who must see before they believe, and those who believe first, and then see the fulfillment of their dreams.

Never share your dreams with people who must see before they believe. They are the secret agents of the Lord of Doubt. Their doubt will poison your mind and possibly derail your dream. Unless the belief and support of such people is crucial to the accomplishment of your goal, don't waste time trying to convince them.

Only share your dreams and aspirations with those whose support and belief you can depend on. Be sure, though, to balance this caution with an openness to honest evaluation and constructive criticism. But such advice must come from those who truly believe in you and your ability to create the manifestation of your dream.

Belief is an essential ingredient in fulfilling a dream, because in order for anything to be accomplished in this world, one must first believe it is possible. People who must see before they believe will never experience true faith or the fulfillment of their dreams. They swear by the adage "seeing is believing," but that old motto is far from the truth. The saying should be amended to, "seeing is recognizing the obvious."

True faith is believing when there is no evidence. It is not faith when you already are looking at something. If you don't see a bridge but step out into the open anyway, you are either exercising extreme faith or exceptional stupidity. If, on the other hand, you see the bridge and declare your belief in it, that is not belief, but merely identifying reality.

Fairy-tale thinkers often defend their philosophy, claiming it is faith. But the test of faith is always the vehicle through which it is exercised. In other words, true faith is always acted upon. You can claim you believe you have a million dollars in the bank all day long, but until you write a check, it's just talk.

One of the most annoying characteristics of the Lord of Doubt is his dependability. You can always depend on him to show up whenever you are considering an improvement in your situation or change in your life. Do you know that, without exception, everyone who has ever achieved anything in this world has heard the same voice of Doubt that you do? The difference between them and the non-achiever is that the achievers do not listen to the voice of Doubt.

Achievers reason that surrender is always an option, so why choose it first? If you would like to invite him in, Doubt will always be at your door, but why do that before you have even tried?

Listening to Doubt is like receiving word that a powerful enemy is on his way to either attack you or receive your surrender, and upon receiving the message, you tender your surrender. But think about this: If your enemy is going to give you the option of surrendering anyway, why not wait a bit and test his strength? You can always surrender later.

If your attitude is that you might as well surrender because you won't be able to defeat your enemy anyway, then you are already defeated. You might say, "But I've seen the army! His soldiers are twice as big as mine and his artillery is far superior, so I know I can't defeat him!"

How do you know? Have you ever fought him? Maybe you can't defeat him today, but what about tomorrow? What about you and your allies? What are your resources?

Incidentally, no matter what you may think, you have not seen this army before. You may have seen a similar situation, problem, or threat. You may have been turned down in a marriage proposal, lost a job, or been rejected in an audition. But even if you have seen a similar army, you have not seen the same situation.

The situation is different because you are different. You are not the same person you were the last time you faced your enemy. You have grown. You have added to your experience and knowledge, and therefore, your perspective is different. The world has also changed since the last time you saw a similar army. Nothing at all is the same. It just looks the same.

Doubt is the last voice you should listen to. Why pay any attention to him? You will always have Doubt. You can find Doubt any time you want him. Listen instead to his noble cousin, the Lord of Belief, who is also whispering in your ear. As you pay attention to him, his voice will grow stronger and so will your courage.

*In order for anything to be
accomplished in this world,
one must first believe
it is possible.*

But you will have to take a stand and choose between doubt and belief. They are like two, large objects which cannot be held at the same time. They are mutually exclusive.

Doubt will keep you hidden in your castle until your enemy overcomes you or you die, never having tested your strength.

Belief will thrust you into the fray, where you will undoubtedly sustain injury. But you will also engage the enemy and hold the possibility of victory in your hand. In short, you will truly live, rather than being entombed forever in doubt.

Belief alone will not bring success. You must combine the Power of Belief with the other powers. Why not engage the Power of Mind, remember that every problem has a solution, and engage your creativity? Why not engage the Power of Action, and at least try before you make up your mind that you can't win? If you do fail, why not engage the Power of Failure to transform your life?

The next time the Lord of Doubt whispers in your ear, why not expel him from your castle? He will surely try again, but just as the voice of the Lord of Belief grows stronger as you listen to him, be confident that the Lord of Doubt's voice grows weaker as you ignore him.

13

THE LORD OF INDULGENCE

The Lord of Indulgence is known as a loud, merry fellow with a boisterous personality. He is always the life of the party and is most often found laughing or wearing a smile which, in truth, more closely resembles a smirk. Everyone likes having him around, perhaps because he so closely resembles his cousin, the Lord of Pleasure.

His motto is "you deserve it," pertaining to whatever amusement you so happen to desire. But make no mistake, the Lord of Indulgence never openly advocates an immoral or decadent lifestyle. Not really. No, he agrees that you must show restraint, get to work, and be disciplined. In fact, he advocates that you represent the very picture of respectability and self control—just not right now.

He tells you that right now you are past due for your share of fun. He is the one whispering in your ear to have one more, even after you just had one more. He is the one beckoning for you to stretch the envelope of pleasure.

One of the principle differences between the Lord of Indulgence and his cousin is how you feel after spending time with each of them. After spending time with the Lord of Pleasure, you feel refreshed and energized, ready for new challenges and opportunities.

Unlike time spent with his cousin, time spent with the Lord of Indulgence leaves you feeling worse, not better. You are more tired, overweight, hungover, or in debt. You need a break from your break.

That irony never seems to bother Indulgence. He always insists that what you really need is more time with him and a bit more fun. But what he conveniently forgets to mention is that any fun that owns you is really slavery.

The hidden second page of the Lord of Indulgence's contract is that there is always a price to pay for his company. In fact, he is the most jealous of all the Lords of Mediocrity, insisting that you spend time with him to the exclusion of any other relationship or responsibility. He never insists on this devotion all at once, but will incrementally own you, if given the chance. If given rein, he will take away your family, your income, your pride, and even your life.

When you are with him, you will notice you are always the one who picks up the tab. Indulgence will spend you into a mountain of debt.

After spending time with him, you will observe that you don't possess the self-confidence you had before. The insecurity you feel will often lead you back to his door.

But the Lord of Indulgence also has a dark mood, and he is glad of your company in those times too. Not only would he have you indulge in enjoyment, he would just as soon have you indulge in such things as self-pity, criticism, and anger. One is just as good as the other to him, since they all lead to the same end: your demise.

Demise? Surely that is too strong a word. All who enjoy the Lord of Indulgence's friendship would think so. His presence is so seemingly innocent, his company so inviting—who would suspect any evil of him?

But many are the lives which he has lain waste. Many people get trapped by their patterns of indulgence, never again to recover.

Sometimes the results are disastrous: a middle-aged man becomes a compulsive gambler, a housewife becomes an alcoholic, a young couple's marriage falls apart under a heavy load of consumer debt. Without exception, all of them thought it could never happen to them.

Sometimes association with the Lord of Indulgence results only in a life of mediocrity, which is really just another type of disaster: the worker who never gets promoted in his menial job, the woman who goes through one dead-end relationship after another—countless lives that will never realize their potential

Subtle are the wiles of the Lord of Indulgence. Like any of the other Lords of Mediocrity, he is never far away. His invitation is always open. Fortunately, though, there is another invitation extended to you, that of the Lord of Pleasure.

Quite unfairly, the Lord of Pleasure is often mistaken for his evil cousin. Perhaps, when you first heard his name, you thought they were one and the same? Not so.

The Lord of Pleasure has a rightful place in your kingdom. He recognizes that everyone has a need for pleasure and knows that life would be dull indeed without him.

The trouble is that both he and the Lord of Indulgence use the same language and, thus, the difference between them is at times difficult to discern. They both say you deserve a break and need to have fun. They both recognize pleasure has its place in your life.

The difference is found in their relationship with discipline, which is the friend of one and despised by the other. Indulgence sees discipline as a threat and nuisance, whereas Pleasure recognizes that the existence of discipline complements and enhances pleasure. Discipline always welcomes Pleasure, but sees Indulgence as a danger to its very existence. You cannot know true pleasure until you have experienced the discipline of fulfilling your obligations and duties.

If you are to avoid the snares of Indulgence, you must assign discipline to vigilantly stand guard against him. No leniency must be shown him at all. Given the slightest chance, he will break his bonds and enslave you again. Employ the Power of Character, using discipline to set boundaries which the Lord of Indulgence must not violate.

If Indulgence has already captured you, you must do everything in your power to wrest yourself from his grip. If you need counseling, then by every means possible, get it. If you need accountability, then seek it out. Reject the fairytale notion that someday you will do something about it. Remember that "someday" never comes.

Don't let your mistakes defeat you. Develop the Power of Failure and use those mistakes to grow stronger. Have you not gained wisdom from your battle with the Lord of Indulgence? Have you not looked into the eyes of your enemy and grown smarter because of errors you have made?

Indulgence would deceive you and have you believe that he is invincible, but the only power he has is that which you give him. Defeating him will certainly not be easy once you have tasted his goods, but many people have escaped his hold. You have the very same powers available to you as those that have conquered Indulgence, but for any of the Seven Powers to work, they must be activated and exercised.

Engage the Power of Belief and know that Indulgence has no claim over you. He was never meant to rule you and can only do so with your consent. Will you allow him to dominate you, or

> *Indulgence would deceive you and have you believe that he is invincible, but the only power he has is that which you give him.*

will take your rightful place as the ruler of your kingdom?

14

THE LORD OF EMOTION

A h, the ever-volatile Lord of Emotion. One moment euphorically happy, the next, melancholy. One moment confident, the next, wracked with fear. One moment passionately in love, the next, passionately spiteful. He laughs. He cries. He broods. He frets. He possesses a never-ending supply of moods from which to choose.

The trouble, of course, is that it is so easy to be swept up in his wake. When he enters the room, you simply must pay attention. If you let him, the Lord of Emotion will grab you by the lapels and speak into your ear until he commands your complete attention.

He is the cousin of the Lord of Feelings and the mortal enemy of Reason. His goal is to grip your heart until you disengage your mind, abandon all reason, and make all your decisions under his influence. Fear, pride, and greed are a few of his favorite tools.

When you are in the process of deciding on an investment, you may assuredly expect him to burst into the room, chattering excitedly about the great wealth this opportunity offers. He might urge you to act hastily, lest this once-in-a-lifetime opportunity disappear. (He is a great proponent of fairy-tale thinking.) You can see the greed in his eyes as he describes this investment in the most lucrative terms, downplaying any risk.

If you are considering changing jobs, it might be that risk is all he talks about. With a furrowed brow, wringing his hands nervously, he will whine about the great hazard this move represents. He will talk endlessly about the security of your present position and imply that failure and humiliation will surely follow any change. Listen to him for just one moment, and before you know it, the Lord of Doubt will also be right by your side, speaking into your other ear.

If you have wronged someone in a significant relationship, the Lord of Emotion will speak only of the wrong you have suffered. Why should you apologize? Let the other person apologize first or, better yet, why apologize at all? Once again invoking the faulty reasoning of fairy-tale thinking, he will most likely recommend that you just forget about any wrong you committed and hope the whole thing is forgotten by the other party.

If you should happen to begin to reason for a moment or two, the Lord of Emotion is not terribly afraid. He knows that nine times out of ten, the emotional argument triumphs over the rational one. He knows that this principle holds true in politics, religion, business, and relationships. All things being equal, in hand-to-hand combat, Emotion almost always beats Reason.

Why? Because while Reason calmly discusses his position, Emotion frantically gestures and raises his voice. He screams and cries as he fervently argues his point. It doesn't matter that he really has little or no rationale behind his argument. He has blind desire and ignorant fear on his side. With these powerful allies, his arguments begin to make sense.

But emotion was never intended to dominate and control your life. On the contrary. It is an enhancement. No one knows this more than the Lord of Feelings. He was there when you were married, when your children were born, when you got a new job, or moved into your first home. He was also there, helping you to grieve, whenever you experienced defeat or lost a loved one. Any time you have rejoiced or grieved, the Lord of Feelings was at your side. Your feelings are what connect you with your world and the people around you.

But the Lord of Emotion will not be satisfied with these limitations. No, he wants to dominate your life. He would have you think that it is right to be battered about by emotion when your life is most chaotic. He would have you match your mood to the tempo of the circumstances in your life. When you encounter turbulent rapids as you float down the river

> *Emotion was never intended to dominate and control your life.*

of life, he would have your mind be as unsettled as the water in which you are traveling. He would have you react to the moment, making rash decisions in the heat of passion, instead of calling on Reason to assist you in your time of need.

While the other Lords of Mediocrity may be dealt with by ignoring them, the Lord of Emotion must be called out and confronted. You must look him squarely in the eye and denounce him for what he is. Anything less will invite his lingering presence. You must call Reason to your aid, but the only way to hear the voice of Reason is to quiet the voice of Emotion.

The Lord of Emotion is a lowly cur and should be commanded to lay down and be quiet. Fairy-tale thinkers believe this is impossible and let unrestrained Emotion bully them all of their lives. The Lord of Emotion has convinced them that, because it is a natural tendency to be led by emotion, then it must follow that it is also good. They don't know, or don't want to believe, that they have the power to control the surging tides of emotion and therefore possess the ability to direct their lives in a positive direction. They don't know that emotion can be controlled using the Power of Choice and is not just something that just happens. Not only can it be controlled, but it can be used in one's favor.

For it is passion that drives a sports team fighting against overwhelming odds. It is passion that fuels the entrepreneur as she faces rejection and defeat. Passion energizes and invigorates, but it must be harnessed and directed. Call Reason to your aid using the Powers of Vision and Mind. Fuel your enthusiasm by daily reviewing your vision and plan.

When the Lord of Emotion comes knocking on your door, redirect his energies toward your goals, instead of being led by his. At first, he will behave as a petulant child, refusing to obey. He will repeatedly wander back to you, attempting to shift the focus back in his direction. But as time passes and as you learn to exercise and strengthen your control, you will find it increasingly easy to dominate the rogue Lord of Emotion.

15

THE LORD OF DISTRACTION

It is impossible to describe the appearance of the Lord of Distraction because he is a master of disguise. One day he appears as worry. The next, he will appear as a relationship. Another, as a new opportunity. Still another, as responsibility. Sometimes he even appears dressed as his noble cousin, Focus.

He is less loud, much smarter, and a great deal more dangerous than his brother, the Lord of Indulgence. He is more dangerous because he is subtle and practices his art of distraction with great proficiency. His tools are limitless and his strength, inexhaustible.

He will tirelessly interrupt you when you are involved in any and every task, splintering your attention, and shattering your concentration. He is constantly tapping you on the shoulder, presenting you with a barrage of queries and statements, all of which, he insists, need immediate attention.

He sounds very intellectual and compassionate with only your best interests in mind, and always has a good reason for his interruptions.

"Don't you think you ought to have a bite to eat?"

"Perhaps it would be a good idea to run those errands now."

"Why don't you check in with your friends to see what they are up to?"

When he barges into your room, you usually find yourself courteously heeding his every word. Yes, the interruption might be an annoyance at first, but his demands seem so appealing or reasonable that you hear yourself telling him you are on your way and will be right there.

But the truth is that his many invasions sap your strength, steal your vision, and derail your focus. Like an expert magician, the Lord of Distraction is a master of misdirection. The very moment you need to be looking in one direction, he will wave his hand or flash something shiny and, all at once, your focus has completely changed.

It's not that he doesn't want you to focus. He just wants you to focus on something else—something other than your vision and plan. Unlike his crude brother, Indulgence, the Lord of Distraction possesses a better quality of tools with which to entice you. When his brother uses a party, he will use responsibility. When his brother uses an obsession, he will select an obligation.

> *Like an expert magician, the Lord of Distraction is a master of misdirection.*

How many times have you been working on your dream when a legitimate concern has served as a distraction? Things such as picking up the children from school, making dinner, or the demands of your job are all obligations which can harpoon your focus and sink your dream.

Think of the countless tools that the Lord of Distraction uses to pull your attention away from achieving your desires. All of them fall into two basic genres of distraction: the external and the internal.

EXTERNAL

- The distraction of worry — How difficult it is to concentrateon creating a better future when the present is bogged down with the cares of the world! It is incredibly hard to focus on your dream when you are bombarded with overdue bills and work deadlines.

- The distraction of busyness — Sometimes it is so easy to be busy just being busy. Busyness can be a distraction because, instead of working on your vision, you are running in circles, performing and completing tasks that mask themselves as accomplishment but in reality are just perpetuating a life of mediocrity.

- The distraction of other opportunities — It is a fact of life that when you are full, it is then that food is most readily abundant. You will find that when you are working on making your dream a reality, a host of other opportunities will knock on your door.

- The distraction of family and friends — You might feel guilty calling family and friends a distraction, but they, too, can pull your concentration away from your goals. Of course, they should be a major part of those goals, but, because of the importance of their relationship to you, you are usually distracted much more easily and often.

- The distraction of play — Everyone needs time to relax but there is a time for play and a time for focus. Play becomes a distraction when you allow your day to be riddled with "mini-vacations," short periods of time when your mind wanders and your focus fragments.

INTERNAL

- The distraction of the past — Both good memories and bad can sidetrack you by dominating your thought life. Memories of past failures and hurts, as well as memories of past triumphs, are only useful in teaching us what to do and what not to do. Some people have ceased to live in the present and dwell in a make-believe world of the past, endlessly reliving past victories and agonies.
- The distraction of opinions — Focusing on other people's opinions, both good and bad, can steal your productivity and energy. In the end, whether someone thinks well or poorly of you has little to do with your overall chance of success.
- The distraction of comparison — In the great game of life, you are only competing against yourself. Some people never realize this and constantly compare themselves, their relationships, and their possessions with those of other people. How sad that they allow their lives to be run by other people and their focus and vitality to be robbed. What would happen if they focused on where they were going and what they were doing instead of what their neighbor was doing? Many foot races have been lost by one runner looking sideways to see how the competition is doing instead of focusing his efforts on improving his own performance.

Although he is powerful, the Lord of Distraction is far from indestructible. The most important weapons with which you can defeat him are found in just three of the Seven Powers.

If you find that Distraction is easily able to steal your focus and misdirect your energy, it is highly possible that you need to spend time honing your Power of Vision.

If you find Distraction has you wandering aimlessly, use the Power of Mind to help add clarity to your direction by using the tool of planning. Just the simple act of scheduling time each day to work your plan can send Distraction packing.

Of course, you will not be able to accomplish this without accessing the discipline found in the Power of Character. Distraction will still tap you on the shoulder, but instead of answering, "Yes sir, I'll be right there," you will learn to respond with, "Yes, I am aware of that, and will get to it in forty-five minutes."

Distraction will whisper into your ear that it is impossible to defeat him—that for other people this may work, but in your life, never! This argument resonates with fairy-tale thinkers who always find an excuse to not even try. Their excuse is that they must attend to the needs of their family and household.

Should you neglect your family and friends? Should you just ignore your bills and job? Should you never play and just work all the time?

Absolutely not! Don't think of prioritizing your tasks and responsibilities as excluding the important things of your life, but as compartmentalizing them. "A place for everything and everything in its place" works not only in organizing your material goods, but in organizing your time as well. The principle trick in gaining victory in this area is to write your schedule down and follow it.

Do not allow the Lord of Distraction to tyrannize you. You are in control of your life, not circumstance. You decide ahead of time when to play, pay the bills, or spend time with your family. There is freedom in order and liberty in structure.

THE LORD OF COMFORT

By far, the most subtle and crafty of the Lords of Mediocrity is the Lord of Comfort. He mocks and perverts the efforts of his good cousin, the Lord of Ease, by stretching a moment of ease into a lifetime of inertia. He is the great friend of Fear.

He is the promoter of passivity, the champion of indecision, and the advocate of procrastination. He is an evil necromancer whose voice is soothing and gentle as he softly whispers poison into your ear. Like Emotion, the Lord of Comfort is also a formidable opponent in argument, but instead of shouting at you, he will defeat you by lulling you to sleep. So powerful are his words that he can cause the most miserable of people to remain in their state of misery by convincing them that it is easier not to change. He has enslaved untold millions with his subtle art.

Suppose you are in a dead-end job that is slowly stealing your vitality and robbing your productivity. Perhaps you desire to search for your dream job or start your own business.

The moment you begin thinking that you will seriously consider making a change, you may expect to hear him whisper, "Getting another job will mean updating your resume. What a tremendous bother!"

"But I hate my job," you reply. "I want to leave!"

"Yes, but your employer is now matching your retirement contribution," you hear Comfort saying.

"That's true," you admit. "But what does that matter if I hate my job?"

"Hate your job? Have you forgotten that you have now earned three weeks of vacation a year?" Comfort argues. "You don't want to lose those."

"That's a good point," you concede. "I don't want to lose all that."

Sensing he now has you on the ropes, Comfort moves in for the final blow. "In fact, leaving this job would be a big mistake. You may never get as good a position again."

"Yes," you agree. "I had better work here a bit longer before I consider making a change."

Your perspective of a restrictive prison has now been replaced with the image of a protective womb. But the problem with wombs is that a womb is not meant to house you indefinitely. It will eventually inhibit growth and ultimately kill you if you fail to graduate to the next stage of life.

It is thus that Comfort robs your motivation and vitality. You have signed a contract, agreeing to be miserable almost every day of your life in return for the illusion of security and comfort. Once you used to dream of conquest and achievement; now you settle for mediocrity. Instead of focusing on living your life to the fullest, you have settled for just staying alive. Instead of good, you have accepted good enough. You have sold out and betrayed the best part of yourself.

Whatever happened to the child that used to dream of doing great things, going to far away places, and experiencing all the wonders of life?

Were you seduced by the words of the Lord of Comfort? Do you recognize his voice? He is an expert singer and uses his lilting voice to sing you into a deep sleep, quieting that uncomfortable feeling inside you that something is desperately wrong.

As you are lying in your boat, quietly floating down the stream of life, he doesn't tell you that a treacherous waterfall is just ahead and the end of the ride is almost over. Instead, he bids that you listen to the waters lapping against the side of your boat. Yes, the boat has gotten small as of late, but it is still quite serviceable, he insists. All the while he sings to you, "Sleep, sleep, for there is still time."

The truth that he hopes you never discover is that the clock is ticking. Your life is passing you by at this very moment. You will never get another chance to do something wonderful with your life. You will never have another opportunity to achieve something great. What would you do if he were not barring your way? What would you attempt if he were not choking your commitment?

The Lord of Comfort's goal is the same as the other Lords of Mediocrity—he would have your very life. Don't be fooled by his mild manner. A gentle, gradual murder is still murder. Whereas Emotion would have you crash and burn, Comfort would suffocate you. When Distraction would have you panic in a blizzard, Comfort would have you fall asleep in the snow.

He uses a misguided sense of morality against you, saying, "Isn't what you have good enough? How ungrateful you must be to desire anything else. Quiet your unholy desires, and be satisfied with what you have!"

But the Lord of Comfort is a hypocrite, for while he is telling you to be content, he is gluttonously devouring your impetus. He will swallow your business and consume your relationships. Then he will have your commitment for dessert.

He is also a blatant liar, posing as his virtuous cousin, the Lord of Ease. The Lord of Ease's job is to provide the occasional oasis in your life, to help you make it from challenge to challenge. It is extremely important that you learn to listen to the voice of the Lord of Ease and take rest on a regular basis. The Lord of Ease knows that the person who burns all day, every day, will certainly burn out.

The problem, as is the case with the other lords, is discerning the difference between his and Comfort's voices. Just as with the Lord of Indulgence, the voice of the evil mixes so easily with that of the virtuous.

To escape the clutch of Comfort, you must exercise the Powers of Choice and Mind, intentionally directing your life by planning your course and mapping your path. You must read books that challenge you to break out of your comfort zone. You must call the Power of Character to your aid and ruthlessly apply self-control and discipline to this area, forcing Comfort out of your life.

Remember, you are the ruler of your kingdom. Don't let Comfort manipulate your natural and wholesome desire for ease by turning it into an affection for easy. You decide when you will have ease in your life and what type of ease you will have.

Will it be a well-earned ease, placed at the end of risk and challenge, or will it be a monotonous, suffocating ease of complacency? Will it be the ease of financial or relational reward, or will it be the ease of a vacant familiarity?

Deep in your heart, you know it is not enough to maintain. It is not enough to let your boat float wherever it will. Boats were made for travel, for exploration, for enjoyment. They are designed to be steered. An unguided boat will always come to ruin or rot.

An unguided boat will always come to ruin or rot.

Where is your boat now? Is it taking you on a meandering, meaningless trip, or are you guiding it on the mission and adventure of a lifetime?

CONCLUSION

There will be those who read this book who will insist on clinging to the illusion. They will concede that much has been said that does indeed have merit, but will insist that the principles outlined in this book are not for them. They will smile and say that such concepts are well and good for others, but their situation is different and therefore, the principles do not apply. Once again, the fairy-tale virus is hard at work in keeping its host enslaved.

It is always easier to believe that someday something wonderful may happen than it is to begin working on making that something happen. It is easier to reject truth than to accept responsibility for changing one's life.

But the message of this book is not that everybody will change, but that everyone can. The book you are now reading was written in the fervent belief that success is available to everyone—that everyone has within him the seed of greatness. There will be those who realize they were not meant to be slaves and will never again surrender themselves to deception. Perhaps you are one of these. Maybe you are one who will use each of your Seven Powers to transform a life of stagnation into an explosion of creativity, action, and strength.

Begin now by resolutely deciding that you are forever finished with all forms of fairy-tale thinking. This philosophy has failed you and does not deserve your respect, affection, or allegiance. In all probability, you have already started to use the Power of Choice to divorce yourself from this viral mind set.

Now begin to develop your Power of Vision. Seek your purpose. Believe that there is a calling for which you are uniquely suited. Augment and expand your Power of Mind by reading every book of substance that you can find. Build your plan and then execute it utilizing the Power of Action. Don't be afraid to fail. When you do fail, know that those who would achieve employ the Power of Failure to step up to the next level. Don't let failure discourage you and steal your Power of Belief. You must believe in yourself, others, and the world in which you live if you are to access the riches this life has to offer. Gird yourself with the Power of Character so that you will have the strength of virtue and honor to fortify your life.

Vigilantly guard against the Five Deadly Enemies. Do not discount the power of any of the Lords of Mediocrity, for stealth is their greatest strength and ignorance is their strongest ally. They are real enemies and will destroy you if given the chance.

Although guarding against the Lords of Mediocrity is indeed a strenuous endeavor, the greatest challenge in your pursuit of growth is to change your perspective. If you can change your perspective, you can change your life.

*The only way perspective
can be retained is to plant it
in an action taken today.
If perspective is the
seed of success, then today
is the ground in which
it must be sown.*

Throughout life, we all experience periodic moments of clarity—perhaps in response to a conversation we've had or a book we've read—and just for a moment a door opens into another universe. For just a moment, we catch a glimpse of the immense landscape of endless possibility.

Perhaps, as you have read this book, you have seen such an image. Maybe you have dared to believe, just for an instant, that you can live the life that you have dreamed. Maybe you realized that there was less separating you from achievement and fulfillment than you previously supposed.

But so often, as a book is laid aside or the memory of a conversation fades, your perspective withers and eventually dies altogether. Like a seed without sufficient sunlight and water, it fails to sprout and produce the increase for which it was designed. We walk away from the vision and forget it like last night's dreams. You must not let that happen. You must capture the strength of that perspective and make it your own.

The only way perspective can be retained is to plant it in an action taken today. If perspective is the seed of success, then today is the ground in which it must be sown.

What action will you take today that will bring you closer to the realization of your aspirations? Will you read a book about finances or relationships? Will you contact a music instructor? Will you begin to research a product idea? Will you open a savings account?

Do not wait for any more signs. Remember that this book is your sign. You must act accordingly. What is the purpose of a sign if it is not to be acted upon? Seize the moment. Capture the enthusiasm you have felt as you have read the words of this book. Transform that energy into momentum.

It is the nature of all life to grow. That which is not growing is dying. Look closely at your life and decide if you will choose to grow, or instead do nothing and die.

Life is certainly not a fairy tale, but it may be that one day your story will be told. It very well may be that someone will even write the story of your life. Will it be a story of extraordinary courage in the face of overwhelming odds? Will it be of an individual who did not accept the lot that had been given him but decided to use the Seven Powers to transform a life of mediocrity?

You are now, in essence, writing your story at this very moment—the very same story that will be told later by another. Why not give all who will one day hear it a tale that will inspire and motivate them? Why not write a story of amazing courage against impossible odds? Why not write of an overcomer who dared the impossible and rose from the ashes to become someone great?

Your story is still being written, and only you can decide how it ends. Only you hold the pen. Begin writing a tale worth telling.

For information regarding
Charles Marshall and M Power Resources, please
visit **www.MPowerResources.com** or
e-mail **info@MPowerResources.com.**